Vol. 2
LIFE OF CHRIST

Theme: God Works Miracles
Six lessons from the Miracle at Cana to the Raising of Jairus' Daughter

Author—Katherine Hershey
Artist—Charles Banse

Contents

Overview of Life of Christ	2
Lesson Seven Miracle at a Wedding (The First Miracle)	3
Lesson Eight Miracle in a Pharisee (Nicodemus Experiences the New Birth	7
Lesson Nine Miracle at Samaria (Samaritans Receive the Living Water)	11
Lesson Ten Miracle Worker—Received and Rejected (Healing of Nobleman's Son, Rejection at Nazareth)	15
Lesson Eleven Miracle Outside Jericho (Blind Bartimaeus Made to See)	19
Lesson Twelve Miracle at Capernaum (Raising of Jairus' Daughter)	23
Song "My God Is So Great," music and visual	28
Additional Review Games	31
How to Lead a Child to Christ	31
How to Lead a Child in Consecration	31
Theme Verse Hebrews 13:8	32
Token Master	Inside back cover

Copyright © 1949, 1959, 1987, 1994 Child Evangelism Fellowship Inc. All rights reserved.
No portion of this book may be reproduced in any form without permission of the publisher.

This CEF PRESS® item was produced by CHILD EVANGELISM FELLOWSHIP® INC. CEF® INC. is a Bible-centered, worldwide, faith organization, composed of born-again believers. Its purposes are to evangelize boys and girls, disciple them in the Word of God and establish them in the local church. This is accomplished through Good News Clubs®, 5-Day Clubs®, fair ministries, camp ministries and related programs. For more information and a descriptive catalog of products, contact your local CEF director or the publisher.

CEF PRESS®
A ministry of Child Evangelism Fellowship® Inc.
Helping You Evangelize Children
WARRENTON, MO 63383-0348

ISBN 1-55976-001-X

An Overview of Life of Christ 2

Lessons have been designed to provide foundational teaching for the child in understanding the Word of God. The stated aim of each lesson is your guide. Use the theme song, "My God Is So Great," each week as suggested in the overview. You may want to emphasize Hebrews 13:8 as a theme verse for the course.

"Jesus Christ the same yesterday, and today, and for ever" Hebrews 13:8.

Lesson	Aim	Verse	Features
Lesson Seven **Miracle at a Wedding** (The First Miracle)	The child may know Christ as the one who can solve his problems.	"Whatsoever he saith unto you, do it." John 2:5	Introduce theme song "My God Is So Great," visuals, pages 28—29. Review game "Dot to Dot" (disciples), page 31.
Lesson Eight **Miracle in a Pharisee** (Nicodemus Experiences the New Birth)	That the unsaved child may see that he comes short of God's standard and needs new life in Christ. That the Christian child may know that a changed life is evidence of his new birth.	"…Except a man be born again, he cannot see the kingdom of God." John 3:3	Continue use of theme song. Substitute "I Believe" (vs. 1) for "A Child's Belief." Review game "Dot to Dot" (disciples).
Lesson Nine **Miracle at Samaria** (Samaritans Receive the Living Water)	That the child may learn to show love and concern for those who are different (physically, racially, morally, socially) from himself.	"…the Spirit and the bride say, Come. And let him that heareth say, Come. And let him that is athirst come…." Revelation 22:17	Theme and "I Believe" songs. "Dot to Dot" Review game (Bible stickers/Bible verses).
Lesson Ten **Miracle Worker—Received and Rejected** (Healing of Nobleman Son, Rejection at Nazareth)	That seeing the contrast between receiving and refusing Christ, the child may choose to receive Him and trust Him to help in time of need.	"He came unto his own, and his own received him not. But as many as received him, to them gave he power to become the sons of God, even to them that believe on his name:" John 1:11, 12	Theme and "I Believe" songs. "Dot to Dot" Review game (Miracles).
Lesson Eleven **Miracle Outside Jericho** (Blind Bartimaeus Made to See)	That the child may learn to know and follow the Lord Jesus as the light of his life.	"…I am the light of the world: he that followeth me shall not walk in darkness, but shall have the light of life." John 8:12	Theme song "My God Is So Great" (vss. 1 and 2). "I Believe" (vss. 1 and 2). "Dot to Dot" Review game (charades), page 31.
Lesson Twelve **Miracles at Capernaum** (Raising of Jairus' Daughter)	That the child may trust the Lord Jesus to use His power to meet needs in his life.	"Jesus Christ the same yesterday, and today, and for ever" Hebrews 13:8	Theme song "My God Is So Great" (vss. 1 and 2). "I Believe" song (vss 1 and 2) "Dot to Dot" Review game (charades). Verse review (Bible ping-pong).

Suggested Aids for Total-teaching hour

Visualized songs: "My God Is So Great" (Vs. 1 pictures mountains, rivers and stars. Vs. 2 pictures cross, open tomb and returning Christ to be pointed to when singing: "Christ died for me; He rose again; He's coming for me I know."), "I Believe"

*Songbooks: Salvation Songs for Children 1, 2, 3, 4 and Growing Songs for Children I and 2

*Visualized Verses • Verse Token Master (inside back cover) • Review Games (described with lessons; additional activities, page 31.)

*Available from CEF Press

LESSON SEVEN

MIRACLE AT A WEDDING
(The First Miracle)

Scripture
John 2:1-11

Aim
That the child may know Christ as the one who can solve his problems.

Memory Verse
John 2:5 — "Whatsoever he saith unto you, do it"

Teaching the Memory Verse
A very special word in this verse is "He." Do you know who HE is? (The Lord Jesus Christ.) Whatever He says is very important. How do we find out what He says? (From the Bible.) His word is God's word, for He is God the Son. (Emphasize here who Jesus Christ is.) Are you willing to do what He says? Willing to obey His word? Sometimes there may not be a Bible verse with a direct answer to your problem.

Visual Aids
A large *zero* makes an impressive visual for use with "There's Nothing Too Hard for Thee."
Use an outdoor and an indoor flannel background with figures 2C-84 — 2C-89.

Suggested Songs
Salvation Songs Number 1: "There Were Twelve Disciples," No. 43; "There's Nothing Too Hard for Thee," No. 65
Salvation Songs Number 3: "God's Word," No. 11; "Trust and Obey," No. 49
Salvation Songs Number 4: "I Have Decided to Follow Jesus," No. 76

Schedule for Teaching
Song — "God's Word"
Song — "There's Nothing Too Hard for Thee" (Discuss things which are not too hard for the Lord Jesus to do for us.)
Song — "I Have Decided to Follow Jesus" (Discuss what it means to *follow* Jesus.)
Teach Memory Verse
Song — "Trust and Obey"
Review Questions (Review time provides opportunity for reinforcing Gospel truths)
Song — "There Were Twelve Disciples"
Lesson — "Miracle at a Wedding"
Application of Truth

Review Questions
1. When the Lord Jesus lived here on earth there were those who followed and learned from teachers and preachers. What were those followers called?
A. Disciples
2. By what name did John the Baptist call the Lord Jesus?
A. The Lamb of God (John 1:29)
3. Why did he call Him the Lamb of God?
A. Because lambs died on the altar for sins and Jesus would die on the cross for sin.
4. What did John the Baptist say Jesus would do with sin that lambs could never do?
A. "Take away the sin of the world" (John 1:29)
5. What was the reason for Andrew's excitement in telling his brother about the Lord Jesus?
A. He believed Jesus was the Messiah (John 1:41)
6. Who did Nathaniel say the Lord Jesus was?
A. The Son of God (John 1:49)
7a. What kind of work did Peter, Andrew, James and John do?
A. They were fishermen (Mark 1:16, 19)

7b. What did Jesus want to make of them?
A. Fishers of men (Matthew 4:19)
8a. Why did people not like Matthew, the tax collector? (Mark 2:14-16)
A. Because tax collectors were often dishonest men (Mark 2:15)
8b. Why did Jesus love Matthew?
A. He loves everyone and came for sinners (I Timothy 1:15; Luke 19:10)
9. What did the Lord Jesus do all night before he chose "the twelve"?
A. He went into the mountain and prayed (Luke 6:12).
10. The twelve men chosen by the Lord Jesus were very different one from the other. What does this teach us?
A. That God loves each one of us and made us like we are. There is something every one of us can do to serve Him.
Have you thought of something you can do well and how you can do it for God?

(Teacher: Take time to discuss this as a follow-up of application of Lesson Six. Be sure to help child who feels he can do nothing, to see what he can do.)

Lesson
Do you sometimes have problems? Are there times when you think, *I wish I knew what to do?* Or, are there times when you know what to do, but, you do not want to do it? Let's say our memory verse!
"Whatsoever he saith unto you, do it" (John 2:5).
Do you think the Lord can help you with your problems?
(Teacher: It will be most effective if you can recall a problem the Lord helped you to solve. The following can be used if you need it.)
A teacher promised to speak to a big group of boys and girls at a rally. Several days before the rally she got a very bad cold. Her throat was sore and then she couldn't talk loud. "Heavenly Father," she prayed, "you know I can't talk to those boys and girls like this. But, this is Your meeting and You will have to solve the problem. Either supply someone else to speak or give me a voice to do it."
Even though she couldn't talk loud she kept planning for the meeting. About twenty minutes before she was to speak her voice was clear. She taught the lesson and after the rally was over, again she could only talk in a whisper!
People had problems at the time the Lord Jesus lived on the earth, too. We learn about one of them today.
Several families in the little town of Cana were planning for a happy time. There was to be a wedding!
I'm sure plans were being made weeks before the wedding day in the homes of both the bride and the groom. There was sewing of wedding clothes. There were discussions as to the wedding guests. There were plans for the wedding dinner. How much food would they need? And, how much wine? There was so much work to be done that perhaps the family almost forgot to be happy about the wedding! But, they knew that when that special day arrived there would be much joy.
Of course, there would be the joy of the bride and groom in their love for one another. But an even more wonderful kind of love is God's love for you and me. His kind of love is the same for every person. The Bible says, "God so loved the *world,* that he gave his only begotten Son . . ." You can enjoy God's love right now. Just believe that He loves you and receive the precious gift of His Son. That will bring you much joy.
The guests at the wedding would be happy because of the happiness of the bride and groom. Also, the guests would enjoy one another. The wedding dinner would be just right. Everyone would be pleased with the delicious refreshments.

Scene 1 (outdoor background)
(Place Nathaniel, figure 2C-84)

Nathaniel, one of the disciples of the Lord Jesus, lived in Cana. Since Cana was a little town, Nathaniel must have known the family, and would have been invited to the wedding. Not only was Nathaniel invited, but the Lord Jesus was invited, too. The Bible says, "Jesus was invited, and also his disciples."
(Place Christ and disciples, 2C-85 and 2C-86)

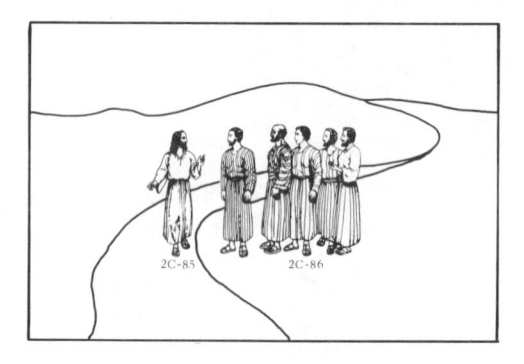

The wedding family may have been relatives of the Lord Jesus, because His mother, Mary, was to be a guest, too. (Since the Bible does not mention Joseph at this time it is possible that he was no longer living.)
(Remove figures)
Finally the important day arrived. The house must have been decorated with flowers and greenery. The main celebration was at evening time so the lamps and candles made it even more beautiful.

Scene 2 (indoor background)
(Place servant, Christ, disciples and Mary, figures 2C-84 — 2C-87)

As the guests arrived they stopped by the big water jars. Because the streets and roads were dusty and people wore sandals, their feet were dirty. A servant was there by the water jars to wash their feet. Then, there was a rule about washing hands so each person had to let the servant pour water over his hands, even if his hands were not dirty. The servants needed big jars filled with water to take care of all that washing!

There were probably children among the guests, skipping to the sounds of happy music. Nuts might be passed around to them even before the main meal began. At last the meal was ready to be served. Trays filled with special foods were passed from person to person. Wine glasses were filled from big pitchers. More and more people were arriving.

(If desired additional figures may be added)

At that time people sometimes went to weddings without a special invitation from the family of the bride or groom. There was a wedding procession, as the bride was taken to the home of the groom where the wedding feast was held. People along the way would join the happy group. One could not be sure just how many people would be there, but everyone was to be served refreshments. That could cause a problem when there were many more guests than expected. This wedding was attended by a great many guests. Again and again the trays and pitchers were filled.

A waiter returned with his empty pitcher. As the servant filled it he asked, "Have most of the guests been served? The wine is nearly all gone."

"Nearly gone?" His voice sounded troubled and his face looked worried. "Many guests have not been served. Whatever can we do?" It was about the worst problem they could imagine!

The word was whispered from one person to another. "There is no more wine."

(Note to teacher: Do not take away from the lesson by trying to explain about the wine. The MIRACLE by the one who can solve life's problems is the aim of the lesson. If children have questions, deal with them on an individual basis, not allowing your class hour to be used to discuss temperance. God did not attempt an explanation.)

Somehow, it seemed just right to Mary to share that problem with her Son. She was sure He would understand. He does understand our problems and He wants us to tell Him about them. He understands about our sin problem, even though He never sinned.

Sin is doing anything that displeases God. Unkindness is sin. Selfishness is sin. Disobedience is sin. We were born with a "want to sin" within us. The Bible says we are held fast with the ropes of our sins (Proverbs 5:22). And, that is a problem, for we cannot set ourselves free. The Lord Jesus was born without a "want to sin" within Him. But, He understands the awfulness of sin. He took *your* sin on Himself when He died on the cross shedding His blood for you (I Peter 2:24). Now He lives again and is waiting to forgive your sin when you trust Him. You never need to be afraid to share your sin problem or any other problem with Him; just as Mary shared the problem about the wine.

The answer of the Lord Jesus to Mary sounds strange to us until we understand what it means. He said, "Woman, what do I have to do with you? My time is not yet come."

It was not unkind of Him to call her "Woman," instead of "Mother." He may have been reminding her that it was more important that people know He was God's Son rather than her son. When He said, "My time is not yet come," He may have been explaining that it was not the time when the crowd at the wedding would believe that He was the Son of God. Cana was not far from Nazareth, where the Lord Jesus grew up, so many folks at the wedding would have known Him from the time He was a little boy. To them, He was "Joseph's son."

Mary may not have entirely understood the words the Lord Jesus spoke to her, but she was trusting Him to do something special. It is wonderful to know He is going to help you with your problem even though you don't understand. Mary believed like that. She turned to the servants.

"Whatsoever he saith unto you, do it," she said, meaning *if you do what He says, He can solve your problem.*

It is our memory verse for today. Let's say it together. (Repeat, "Whatsoever he saith unto you, do it" John 2:5)

The servants looked at Him. What would He say? He may have pointed to the six big water jars. "Fill the jars with water," He said.

(Exchange figure of Christ 2C-85 for 2C-89)

The servants probably thought, It would be very strange to fill the jars now. Why should we fill the jars after the guests are all here? "Whatsoever he saith unto you, do it." Even though they could not understand why, they did it. They filled the jars up to the brim — all six of them.

"Now, take some out," He said, "and serve it to the manager of the feast." (The manager would be like the headwaiter, or the man in charge)

They must have hesitated, wondering why they should serve water to the manager. But then, *whatsoever he saith unto you . . .* They obeyed. They filled their pitchers. They could not believe what they saw. It was *wine!* They hurried into the dining room to the manager. They served him and waited to see what would happen when he tasted the new wine. He did not know the first was all gone, so he would not be expecting anything unusual. They watched as he took one sip. He looked surprised. He drank a bit more, and he looked very pleased.

Paying no attention to the servants the manager went right to the groom. "Where did you get this?" he asked. "I've never known anyone to serve the best wine last. Everyone serves the best first and keeps that which is not so good until last when people have really had enough to eat and drink. But, this is the best!" It was very likely the best he had ever tasted. And no wonder. It was created by the Lord Jesus Himself.

A problem was solved by a miracle. And so it can be for you. You may be thinking, *I never saw a miracle.* Do you know that the greatest miracle *ever* is that you can have your sins forgiven and become a child of God? You can live forever with the Lord Jesus, because He rose from the dead, and will give you everlasting life. Has that miracle happened in your life? If not, it can happen right now. You can talk to the Lord Jesus something like this:

"Lord, I know sin is a problem in my life. I want to be set free from my sin. Thank You for dying to take care of it. Right now I receive You and trust You to save me from my sin."

If you did pray that prayer just now or would like to know more about receiving the Lord Jesus, I would like to talk with you after class. Perhaps you have received the Lord Jesus before? If so, thank Him again for the miracle He did in your life when you trusted Him to save you from sin.

The Bible says this was the first miracle performed by the Lord Jesus, and that through it He showed His glory, or His glorious power. Also, it says, "His disciples believed in Him." Did they not believe in Him before? Surely they did. This means that they were more certain than ever that He was the

Messiah, the promised one of God. The miracle of turning water into wine made their belief even stronger.

Nathaniel must have remembered the day when the Lord Jesus told him that He knew all about him, and then added, "You will see greater things than these." This was the beginning of those greater things.

What about the other people? Did they believe? Probably most of them did not. Surely they heard about the miracle. They may have just wondered about it, not trusting the Lord Jesus as God's Son. They were not ready to turn their problems over to Him.

What about your problems? Do you believe the Lord can help you with them? Some of you are not so sure about that. Your problem seems so big and you do not understand how He could possibly help. What does He want you to do, so that He might help you?

He wants you to tell Him about the problem. In I Peter 5:7 it says you are to cast your care upon Him, "for he careth for you." That means just tell Him all about it. Sometimes it may be well to share your problem with other Christians so that they can pray for you, too. "Whatsoever he saith unto you, do it."

Do you have a problem that you would like to share with us today? There may be an answer in God's Word that we can find right now — something that God would tell you to do. Or, we may have to wait for awhile to find the answer.

(Teacher: Give opportunity for sharing, and be much in prayer for any help you may be able to give. If group does not respond, pose the problems listed here or similar ones for them to solve. Encourage them to think of problem situations where the Lord can help them during the next week, and to be ready to respond at the next class session. Do not be above sharing some problem of your own. May we be in constant prayer that our teaching becomes practical in the lives of our children. Close session with prayer after giving instruction to those who would like to receive the Lord Jesus as Saviour where they should meet you for counseling)

Sing: "There's Nothing Too Hard for Thee"

PROBLEMS THE CHILDREN MAY SOLVE FROM GOD'S WORD

Several solutions are posed for the problems. Ask children to decide which thing the child should do. Read the Scriptures to find God's answers.

Johnny needed new shoes. His old ones were worn out. There was not enough money after groceries and rent for him to have new ones. What should Johnny do?

— Worry
— Steal
— Expect God to supply
— Be angry
— Be thankful

Bible verses: Matthew 6:25-33; Ephesians 5:20

Mike was very ill in the hospital. The doctor said as a result of his illness he would never be able to walk. Mike had wanted to be a missionary pilot when he grew up. What should he do?

— Demand that God make him able to walk again
— Trust God to show him what to do
— Expect God to heal his legs
— Thank God that He knows best

Bible verses: Proverbs 3:5, 6; Romans 8:28; II Thessalonians 5:16-18

LESSON EIGHT

MIRACLE IN A PHARISEE
(Nicodemus Experiences The New Birth)

Scripture
John 2:13-16, 23; 3:1-16; 7:44-52; 19:39-42; Numbers 21:5-12

Aims
That the unsaved child may see that he comes short of God's standard and needs new life through Christ
That the Christian child may know that a changed life is evidence of his new birth

Memory Verse
John 3:3 — "...Except a man be born again, he cannot see the kingdom of God"

Teaching the Memory Verse
This verse really needs to be explained in the context of the lesson so teach it at that point rather than before the lesson.

Visual Aids
Flannel backgrounds: Plain, temple and housetop scenes with figures 2C-90—97. Place figure 2C-97, serpent on pole, on small board or on a flannel inset on your scene showing the discussion between the Lord Jesus and Nicodemus.

To visualize the words in the last paragraph of lesson indicating a changed life (courage, love, obey, kind, helpful, truthful), use newsprint and marking pen. Cut paper doll figures for boys and girls in club to be used on large poster for lesson application. Print names of children below dolls on chart.

"A Child's Belief," visualized hymn, is available from Bible Visuals, Inc. P. O. Box Z, Akron, Pennsylvania 17501.

Suggested Songs
Salvation Songs Number 1: "There's Nothing Too Hard for Thee," No. 65; "John 3:16," No. 7 (or use variation suggested under *Salvation Songs Number 3*)
Salvation Songs Number 2: "The Gospel," No. 95; "Just Like Nicodemus," No. 92
Salvation Songs Number 3: "A Child's Belief," No. 5; "For God So Loved the World," No. 38

Schedule for Teaching:
Song — "A Child's Belief"
Song — "The Gospel"
Prayer
Review Questions
Song — "There's Nothing Too Hard for Thee"
Song — "John 3:16" or "For God So Loved..."
Lesson — "Miracle in a Pharisee"
Song — "Just Like Nicodemus"
Application of Truth

Review Questions
1. At what special place did we find the Lord Jesus in our lesson last time?
A. At a wedding
2. Who were some others who were at the wedding beside the Lord Jesus?
A. His mother, Mary; Nathaniel; and other disciples.
3. Why did they need the big water jars at the wedding?
A. The hands and feet of the guests were washed when they arrived.
4. Perhaps more guests came to this wedding than those who were invited by the families of the bride and groom. What big problem did this cause?
A. There was not enough wine.
5. When Mary learned about this, what did she do?
A. She told the Lord Jesus.
6. Why was that a good thing to do?
A. The Lord Jesus can help us with our problems if we share them with Him.
7. What did Mary tell the servants?
A. "Whatsoever he saith unto you, do it."

8. What did the Lord Jesus tell the servants to do?
A. "Fill the water jars with water."
9. What happened when they did that?
A. When the water was poured from the jars it was turned to wine.
10. The Bible says this was the first miracle performed by the Lord Jesus. What great miracle can He perform for you?
A. He can forgive sin, and make us children of God, because He died for us.

Discussion question regarding last lesson:
What problem did you have last week and how did the Lord help you? (Encourage discussion here.)

Lesson
The story is told of Mr. Crow who was tired of being a crow and wanted to be a pigeon. He tried to walk and talk like a pigeon. He covered himself with gray dust to look like a pigeon. But when it rained the gray washed off and the pigeons knew he was a crow!

Another funny story tells about a monkey who is supposed to have crawled inside a lion skin and pretended he was a lion. But, when a tiger came along he was proven to be just a scared monkey instead of a brave lion!

Have you ever thought it would be fun to be something other than what you are? Or, maybe you've wanted to be some other person than yourself! (Involve pupils in *brief* discussion.)

Some people do a lot of pretending. Some pretend to be rich. Some pretend to be brave. Some pretend to be good. It is not too hard to fool or deceive other people with our "pretendings," but we can never deceive God. He knows everything about us.

Scene 1 (plain board)
(Place Nicodemus, figure 2C-90)

Nicodemus was a man who lived and worked among many pretenders. Nicodemus was a Pharisee. The Pharisees were men who lived at the time the Lord Jesus lived on the earth. They pretended to be very good. Some of them did seem to the people who knew them to be good. But, none of them was as good as God is good. The Bible says, "All have sinned and come short of the glory of God," or of God's goodness. Do you sometimes compare yourself with others? But, do you measure up to God's goodness? No! You and I are sinners.

Nicodemus was known to most people as a "good Pharisee." He lived in the city of Jerusalem. He had probably heard about John the Baptist, for many of the Pharisees went to see what John was doing. John the Baptist told them to "stop being pretenders." Nicodemus would have heard about the Lord Jesus, too. But, since he was in Jerusalem and the Lord Jesus Christ was in Galilee, Nicodemus did not know much about Him.
(Remove Nicodemus)

Scene 2 (plain board)
(Place Christ, figure 2C-91)

Then, the time of year for the Passover arrived and the Lord Jesus came to Jerusalem. (Do you remember another Passover time when He was in Jerusalem? How old was He then? Yes, he was twelve years old. He is over thirty years old now. Do you think He was in Jerusalem for other Passovers between the age of 12 and 30? He surely must have been and no one noticed Him as being someone special. But, things were different now!) People were beginning to know that the Lord Jesus was no ordinary man. The miracle at the wedding caused much excitement. People watched Him. Those who came from Galilee for the Passover told what they knew. Nicodemus must have learned who Jesus was and watched Him, too.
(Remove figure of Christ)

The temple area was a busy place at Passover time. People, people everywhere. There were the money-changers. A special kind of money was needed in the temple so they exchanged the regular money for temple money. Often the money-changers cheated in exchanging the money.

Scene 3 (plain board or temple scene)
Lambs and bulls and doves were for sale at the temple. The people bought these animals for their sacrifices. Many of the prices for the animals were not fair. Not only was there buying and selling, but there was shouting and arguing.
(Place figures Christ, money-changers, animals and salesmen, 2C-92 — 2C-96)

Suddenly the Lord Jesus was in the middle of all the confusion and He took charge. He snapped a whip rope in the air.

"Take these things out of here," He ordered. "Don't use my Father's house for a market."

Money tables overturned. Coins rolled in every direction. Sheep and oxen ran. Men grabbed cages filled with doves. Nicodemus must have been among those who saw it all happen.

Questions popped from one group to another. "Who is He?" "What does He mean, 'My Father's house'?" "Does He have the right to do such things?"

Nicodemus listened; he asked some questions. In his heart Nicodemus knew this man was someone special. *(Remove figures)*

The Lord Jesus Christ did some miracles in Jerusalem, too, though we are not told what kind of miracles He did at that time. The Bible says many believed in His name when they saw the miracles He did. Only it was sort of a "pretend belief." And, the Lord Jesus knew it. God's Word says, "he knew what was in man." That means He knows all about them. He knows the truth about you, too!

Nicodemus wanted to learn more about this one who seemed to know all about everyone. There must be some way he could talk with Jesus. Nicodemus thought and planned. He learned where the Lord Jesus was staying. And, he planned for a nighttime visit. The Lord Jesus would be alone at night and would have time to talk. Then, too, other Pharisees would not see Nicodemus go at night. The Pharisee crowd was not friendly with Jesus.

Scene 4 *(housetop or plain board)*
(Place figures 2C-90 and 2C-91, Nicodemus and Christ)

Nicodemus probably met the Son of God on the flat housetop of the home where He stayed. The housetop was used as the guest room. "Rabbi (Teacher)," Nicodemus said, "We know you are a teacher who has come from God; for no one could do the miracles you do unless God is with him."

Was the Lord Jesus a teacher? Did He come from God? Was He any more than a teacher from God?

Yes, He was. He was God. . . God the Son.

The Lord Jesus spoke to him in the words of our memory verse.

"Except a man be born again, he cannot see the kingdom of God." *(Place words on board.)*

The kingdom of God would be that over which God ruled. In this verse it seems to mean something like the family of God. Let's repeat the verse together. (Repeat John 3:3) Are there any words that sound strange to you in that verse? Those words sounded strange to Nicodemus.

"How can a man be born when he is old?" he asked. "Surely he cannot become a little baby and be born all over again, can he?"

"It is a different kind of birth from that," Jesus said. "That is the birth of the body. I am talking about the spirit being born new."

The spirit is the part of us which can love and praise and worship God. Until one receives the Lord Jesus, the Bible says that spirit is dead in sin even though the body is alive. When God made the first man and woman He made them with spirits that were alive to God. From their beginning they loved and praised and talked with God. But, when they obeyed Satan and disobeyed God their spirits died, even though their bodies lived many more years. Every person born into the world since that time has a spirit that is dead to God. (That is why it is easier to do wrong than right.) Only God can make your spirit alive. When God, by His Holy Spirit, makes your spirit alive, you are "born again."

"Don't be surprised that I said, 'You must be born again," the Lord Jesus said.

Perhaps on the housetop a cool breeze blew through the trees.

"You hear the wind blowing," the Lord Jesus continued, "and you do not know where it comes from or where it is going. You can't see the wind, but you can see what it does. That is the way it is with everyone who is born again; born of the Holy Spirit."

When you are born in God's family you become a different kind of person. Just as you can see things change because of the wind so your life shows changes because you are born again by the Holy Spirit. Before being born again you might enjoy doing wrong things. But after you are born again you are unhappy when you do something wrong. Before, you would enjoy saying mean things, being unkind, doing anything to have your own way. After being born again, you want to be kind and unselfish. This is because God the Holy Spirit has made a change in you. He reminds you when you do wrong. He gives you a desire to do right. That is really a miracle!

Some people believe it is possible to live in a way that pleases God without being born again. They do many good things and often their lives look as good as those who have been born again. But, their spirits have never been made alive by the Holy Spirit and the good things they do, do not really count with God. They are like the "pretenders" we talked about.

A crow's pretending to be a pigeon could not make him a pigeon. He would have to be born a pigeon. A monkey's pretending would not make him a lion. He would have to be born a lion. And, pretending to belong to God's family by being good does not make one a child of God. He must be born into God's family.

Nicodemus did not pretend he knew what the Lord Jesus was talking about, when he did not. "How can these things be?" he asked the Son of God. He was probably thinking that the Lord Jesus still had not explained *how* to be born again.

"You are a teacher of Israel (a teacher of the Jews) and you don't understand?" the Lord Jesus asked. And then, by reminding him of something which had happened to the children of Israel long before, Jesus told him just how to be born again.

Hundreds of years before the Jewish people were traveling from Egypt to the land God was going to give them. They grumbled and complained and were angry with their leader, Moses. God was displeased and sent poisonous snakes among the people. Many people died from the snakebites and many others were dying.

"Moses," they cried, "ask God to take the snakes away." Moses prayed for the people.

God heard his prayer and made a way for those who were bitten to be healed. He told Moses to make a snake of brass and lift it up on a pole.

(Place figure 2C-97, serpent on pole, on small board or on flannel inset)

"Whoever looks at the snake of brass will be healed," God said. And, they were.

Listen to the words of the Lord Jesus to Nicodemus. "As Moses lifted up the serpent in the wilderness, even so must the Son of man be lifted up: That whosoever believeth in him should not perish, but have eternal life."

What name did the Lord Jesus call Himself in this verse? (Son of man) He often referred to Himself by this name.

What do you think He meant when He talked about being "lifted up"? He meant He would be lifted up on the cross.

Just as the snakebite brought death to those people, so sin has brought death to the spirit of every man, woman, boy and girl. Just as they had been given life through looking at the snake on the pole, so our spirits (the part of us which can love, worship and praise God) are made alive forever (born again) through believing that the Lord Jesus died on the cross for our sin, and receiving Him as our Saviour from sin.

The next words are perhaps the most wonderful in all the Word of God. "For God so loved the world that he gave his only begotten Son, that whosoever believeth in him should not perish but have everlasting life."

Because of God's great love He did not want our spirits to remain dead — separated from Him. So, He gave us His only Son. On the cross the Lord Jesus was separated from the Father when He paid for our sin. We just believe that and trust Him to give us everlasting life. Have you ever been born again? If you have received the Lord Jesus, you have been. If you have not received Him you need to do that. Will you do it this very day? I want to talk with you about it after class so that you may know for sure that you are born again, born into God's family (John 1:12, 13).

(Remove figure 2C-97)

It may have been that very night when Nicodemus was born again. We know he was born again because of his changed life.

(Remove figures from board, holding Nicodemus in hand as you continue)

Some time after Nicodemus had met with the Son of God, the Pharisees were planning to have the Lord Jesus Christ arrested. They had no good reason for doing it, of course. God gave Nicodemus courage to speak up. "Does our law condemn a man without giving him a chance to defend himself?" he asked.

The Pharisees were angry with Nicodemus for saying that. They said some mean things to him but they did not arrest the Lord Jesus at that time.

The last time the Bible speaks about Nicodemus is after the Lord Jesus died on the cross.

The disciples had all disappeared. They were hiding for they were afraid of the Pharisees and others who had crucified the Lord Jesus. It was Nicodemus who brought spices and, with his friend Joseph, wrapped the body of the Lord Jesus in linen and buried it in the garden tomb.

This was a dangerous time to show that he loved the Son of God. But Nicodemus no longer cared what those Pharisees thought of him. He may have been afraid of what they thought the night he came to the Lord Jesus. But, now he was changed. God had given him *courage*. How excited Nicodemus must have been only three days later when he learned the news that Jesus rose from the dead. He was ready to let everyone know of his love for his Saviour, the Lord Jesus Christ.

If you have received the Lord Jesus, your life, too, will be different from what it was before you received Him. You need to think about that. If you say you have been born into God's family and your life has not changed you may be just a "pretender." If you have received the Lord Jesus, God's Word says you have received *new* life. Ask God to help you show others by the things you do and say that your life has been changed. Can you think of some ways your life should be different?

Maybe, like Nicodemus, you need *courage* to speak up for the Lord Jesus among those who do not love Him. You need to show that you *love* Him. It may be that you need to ask God to help you *obey* or to be *kind* and *helpful* and to always tell the truth. Tell Him where you need special help. Trust Him to change you by His Spirit. God's Word says, "The fruit of the Spirit is love, joy, peace. . ." (Galatians 5:22,23). As you trust God to work in you, He will make these things show in your life. Others will see your life is different. To help us this week, I am going to ask each of you to think of one thing you would like God to help you change in your life. We'll write it on a picture above your name and place it on our big poster. There's a place on your memory verse token to write this same thing as a daily reminder.

(After completing this project, close in prayer asking the children first to silently ask God to help them in this week. After prayer, remind them that next week you will discuss together how the Lord answered in helping them. Use your poster again next week.)

(Remind children desiring to receive Christ where to meet you for counsel.)

LESSON NINE

MIRACLE AT SAMARIA
(Samaritans Receive The Living Water)

Scripture
John 4:3-34; 39-42

Aim
That the child may learn to show love and concern for those who are different (physically, racially, morally, socially) from himself.

Memory Verse
Revelation 22:17 — "The Spirit and the bride say, Come. And let him that heareth say, come. And, let him that is athirst come..."

Teaching the Memory Verse
Do you like to receive invitations? Perhaps it's an invitation to a party printed on pretty paper. Or, maybe just a quick invitation that says, "Come for lunch." Or, perhaps your friend says, "Come overnight."
Our verse is an invitation. It is the very last invitation in the Bible — an invitation to a place God has prepared for His children. (Teacher: Show children the location from your Bible relative to the end of Revelation.) Who is doing the inviting? God the Holy Spirit and the bride. Who is the bride? It is all those who have trusted the Lord Jesus for forgiveness of sins. I am part of the bride. Are you?
The invitation is "Come." Where are people invited to come? This chapter of our Bible describes the place where the Lord Jesus is. The place is Heaven...come to Heaven! Receive the Lord Jesus and live with Him forever! Let everyone who has heard and received Him say, "Come!"
Do you know what it means to be thirsty? For our bodies, a cold drink satisfies that thirst. But to satisfy the thirst of the "real you" to know God, you must come and receive the Lord Jesus as your Saviour from sin. You and I need to invite those who are thirsty to come. God's Word says, "Whosoever will may come."

Visual Aids
Flannel background: plain board and outdoor scene; figures 2C-98 — 2C-110. Map, figure 2C-98 has divisions marked by color. You may further indicate divisions by printing names on flags and taping flags to straight pins.
For application, prepare emblems with word "Come" which children may wear this week inviting others to "Come" to Christ or to club, as explained at conclusion of lesson. You may also wish to provide the child with printed invitations he may give out this week as an invitation to your club.

Suggested Songs
Salvation Songs Number 1: "John 3:16," No. 7; "There Were Twelve Disciples," No. 43; "Come to the Saviour," No. 21 (verse 1 only; omit chorus)
Salvation Songs Number 2: "Just Like Nicodemus," No. 92
Salvation Songs Number 4: "I Have Decided to Follow Jesus," No. 76.

Schedule For Teaching
Song — "John 3:16"
Song — "Just Like Nicodemus"
Teach Memory Verse
Song — "Come to the Saviour"
Review Questions
Song — "I Have Decided to Follow Jesus"
Song — "There Were Twelve Disciples"
Bible Lesson — "Miracle at Samaria"
Application of Truth

Review Questions

1. What kind of people were the Pharisees?
A. They pretended to be good and most of them thought they were better than other people.
2. What was the name of the Pharisee who wanted to talk with the Lord Jesus?
A. Nicodemus.
3. What did the Lord Jesus do in the temple that caused lots of excitement?
A. He chased out the money-changers, the animals and those who sold them.
4. When Nicodemus met Jesus at night, who did he think Jesus was?
A. A teacher come from God.
5. Was Jesus more than that?
A. Yes, He was God the Son.
6. What strange thing did Jesus tell Nicodemus?
A. John 3:3, "Except a man be born again, he cannot see the kingdom of God."
7. What did Nicodemus say that showed he did not understand what it meant to be born again?
A. How can a man be born when he is old?
8. Jesus reminded Nicodemus of a story about people who were bitten by poisonous snakes. How were they healed?
A. By looking at a brass snake on a pole.
8b. Why do we need to trust Jesus who was lifted up on a cross?
A. To save us from our sin.
9. John 3:16 tells how to be born again. Who can say this verse?
A. For God so loved the world that he gave his only begotten Son, that whosoever believeth in him should not perish but have everlasting life.
10. How do we know Nicodemus was born again?
A. We know from his changed life.
Sing: "I Have Decided to Follow Jesus"
Have you been following Him? Last week we thought about how our lives are changed by being born again. (Bring out chart made last week) Did God help you change that thing in your life which you wrote down since we were here last time? (After discussion sing: "There Were Twelve Disciples")

Lesson

Ricardo and his family had just moved into the vacant house on Elm Street. Ricardo wondered about making friends. He had many friends in the big city. His friends there liked the same things he liked. They ate the same kinds of food. They enjoyed the same games. They even looked much alike. Here everything was different. Ricardo's skin was darker than that of his neighbors. It was easier for him to say, "Si," instead of "Yes." And "Gracias," instead of "Thank you." He liked tortillas better than French fries. Ricardo rather expected to see his new neighbors keep their distance from his house. Perhaps they would even cross to the other side of the street rather than get too close.
Suppose you had been Ricardo's neighbor . . . what would you have done? How would you feel if everyone else on Elm Street decided to just ignore Ricardo? *(Initiate some discussion here. Wait for answers.)* Could the Lord Jesus give you His love for Ricardo?
There were some people who lived in the land where the Lord Jesus lived who were not liked by their neighbors. The country was in three parts.

(Show map, figure 2C-98)

The northern part was Galilee. That was where the Lord Jesus grew up, and where He began His work. The southern part was Judea. The city of Jerusalem was there, with the temple of God. Most of the leaders of the Jewish people lived in Judea.
The middle part was Samaria. The people of Samaria were not liked by those in Judea and Galilee. When the Jews from Judea went to Galilee, even though it was further they crossed the river and went into another country. They did not want to go through Samaria. (Point out on map)
How do you think the Lord Jesus felt about the people of Samaria? Surely, He loved them. The Lord Jesus did what was right whether anyone else did it or not. He was the perfect Son of God. He did not ignore the Samaritans.

Scene 1 (outdoor)
(Place Christ and disciples, figures 2C-99 and 2C-100)

One day the Lord Jesus and His disciples were on their way from Judea to Galilee. The disciples were probably very much surprised when their leader said something like this, "Today we are going through Samaria."
It may have been a hot day. It was a long walk. When they reached a famous well, just outside the city of Sychar, the Lord Jesus stopped to rest. He was very tired.
"We will go into the city," the disciples said, "and buy some food for our dinner."
(Remove figure of Christ)

Scene 2 (outdoor)
(Place city and woman, figures 2C-101 and 102)

On their way into the city the disciples may have seen a woman from the city coming toward the well with her water jar. Perhaps she glanced at them, but hurried on. Her first thought upon seeing them would have been, *What are those*

12

Jewish men doing here? Well, no matter. She must hurry to the well to get her water.
(Remove disciples)

Scene 3 (outdoor)
Her thoughts were not happy thoughts. There was much unhappiness in her life. Her unhappiness was because of sin. Because she was a sinner, she did many wrong things (Romans 5:12). Sin always brings unhappiness. When you lie and cheat and disobey . . . when you are mean and selfish . . . do these things bring happiness? You may be happy in sin for a while, but not for long. Since sin is displeasing to God, He does not want you to be happy in sin.

Who has sinned? Is anyone perfect? God's Word says, "The Lord looked down from heaven . . . to see if there were any that did . . . seek God. They are all gone aside . . . there is none that doeth good, no not one" (Psalm 14:2,3). Yes, all have sinned. The woman on the way to the well knew she was a sinner.

She would be alone at the well. She was sure of that. Most of the women enjoyed going to fill their water jars. For them it was a good place to meet and talk, and to learn all the news. Perhaps there were times when this woman came in sight that the other women suddenly stopped talking. *"Gossips!"* she may have said to herself, *"I know that they are talking about me."*

Have you ever said the kind of things about someone that made you stop talking when that person came in sight? If you did it was probably because you thought that person was not as good, or as important, as you. The Bible says if you treat some people as though they are not as good as others, or even as good as yourself, you are sinning (James 2:9). You need to trust the Lord Jesus to give you His love for everyone.

The woman knew when the others went for water, so she was careful to go when no one else would be there.

Scene 4 (outdoor)
(Place Christ at well, figures 2C-103 and 104)

But, how surprised she was when she reached the well! She was not going to be alone. There was a man there. She would just get the water and pay no attention to Him. Taking her water jar from her shoulder she may have tried to look the other way.
(Remove woman, 2C-102; replace with 2C-105; place jar, 2C-106 over her right hand, attaching yarn)

She fastened the jar to the rope. Down . . . down into the well. There, it was full of water. Up . . . up from the well. Unfasten the rope, and onto her shoulder, and she was ready to go.

Just at that moment the stranger spoke to her! "Give me a drink."
(Remove 2C-105; place 2C-102)

The woman turned and looked at Him. He was a Jew! A Jew speaking to her . . . a Samaritan woman! Even asking a favor of her. What Jew would ever ask a favor of a Samaritan? (If you consider another person not to be as good, or important, as you, you would not likely ask a favor of him.)

And so, she asked Him. "How is it that you, a Jew, would ask a drink of me, a Samaritan?" She thought He surely knew that Jews would have nothing to do with Samaritans.

"If you knew the gift of God," He said, "and who it is who asked you for a drink, you would have asked Him for a drink and He would have given you living water."

She did not understand what He was talking about and her reply showed it. "Sir, you do not have anything with which to draw water (no water jar)," she said, "and the well is deep. Where can you get this living water? Are you greater than the man who gave us this famous well?"

Was He greater than that man? Of course He was. He was greater than any man who ever lived for He was the only Son of God. But, what did He mean when He talked about the gift of God and living water?

The Bible says, "God so loved the world that He *gave* His only begotten Son . . ." (John 3:16). The world included the Samaritan woman, and it includes you and me. God loved and gave. His *gift* was Jesus, His Son. God gave His Son to die on the cross for our sins. At another place the Bible says, ". . . the gift of God is eternal life . . ." (Romans 6:23). And at still another place, "God hath given us eternal life and this life is in His Son" (I John 5:11). The Lord Jesus had not yet died on the cross. But after shedding His blood, dying on the cross, and being dead for three days, the Son of God rose from the dead. So, the gift of God is the Lord Jesus Himself and when you receive Him you have eternal life.

What about the living water? When you are thirsty you have a need. Water satisfies that need. Every person has a need for forgiveness of sins and eternal life. The Lord Jesus Christ can satisfy that need forever, as water satisfies your thirst. The Lord Jesus tried to make the woman understand.

"Everyone who drinks of this water will get thirsty again," He said, looking at her water jar. She understood that. But, He was not finished. "Anyone who drinks of the living water I have to give will never get thirsty again. It will be like a spring of water within him bubbling up into everlasting life."

"Give me this water," she said, "so that I will not get thirsty again. And, I will not have to come to the well to get water."

She still did not understand that He was not talking about water which would satisfy the needs of her body. But He was talking about satisfying the thirst of the *real you.* The YOU that loves or hates; that feels sad or happy; that wants and wishes and cares. The water in the well could satisfy the need of a thirsty body. The Lord Jesus, forgiving sin and giving eternal life, could satisfy the need of the real YOU.

It was hard for the Samaritan woman to believe that He cared so much about her. He wanted to make sure she did understand. "Go, call your husband," He told her, "And come back here."

Ohh! Those words took her thoughts away from the water in the well. "I have no husband," she answered.

"I know," the Lord Jesus replied. "You have had five husbands and the man you are living with now is not your husband."

Immediately the woman began to think about the sinful life she was living. Now, she began to understand. She had tried to find happiness in many ways. Even with five different husbands! Perhaps she thought, *There is no way to be satisfied and happy.*

Did you ever think if you had one thing more; or if you could go to a special place; or do a special thing; that you would be satisfied? If you have the Lord Jesus to share your life you really do not need a lot of other things to bring you joy and make you satisfied.

By now the Samaritan woman was really puzzled. How did this man know so much about her? How did He know about her sin? "I see you are a prophet," she said. She thought of a prophet as one who knew many things, even things in the future. She wanted Him to know that she knew about God, too, so she told Him. "Our ancestors say that the place to worship God is on this mountain." She probably pointed to the nearby mountain. "You Jews say the place to worship

God is in Jerusalem."

The Lord Jesus was so kind as He talked to her. "The important thing about worshiping God is not *where* we worship," He explained. "The important thing is *how* we worship. We must worship Him in spirit and in truth." He meant that the woman could not pretend she was not sinful and still worship God. She could only worship God with a true and honest heart. God knew her sin and she would have to admit her sin to Him.

She wondered how He knew so much. She spoke again. "I know that when Messiah comes, the one who is called Christ; I know that when He comes He will tell us everything."

"I am He," the Lord Jesus said, "the very one who is talking to you."

The woman asked no more questions. She had no words to say. She knew He spoke the truth, and she just believed . . . with all her heart! Oh joy! How could this have happened to her, a sinful Samaritan woman! She forgot her water jar and hurried back to the city.

(Place 2C-106 on well; remove 2C-102 and place 2C-107, woman)

Scene 5 (outdoor)

Has the Lord Jesus been talking to you during this lesson? Perhaps down deep inside you've been thinking about your sin. Perhaps you have been thinking that you need Him in your life. He wants you to receive Him. You must admit you have sinned, believe that He died and rose again to forgive your sin; then, just tell Him what is on your heart and invite Him to be your Saviour. Let us bow our heads and close our eyes.

You can receive the Lord Jesus right where you are, but I would like to help you. If you have received Him today, or would like to but don't really understand how, will you raise your hand, so that I may know? I want to talk with you after class.

(Remove 2C-107)

Scene 6 (outdoor)

It was strange for a Jewish teacher to speak with a woman, other than his family, in that time. To speak to a Samaritan woman, one whom people knew as a sinful woman, was still more strange. But, these things made no difference to the Lord Jesus. Things like the way people look or dress, or talk, or where or how they live should make no difference to us who know the Lord Jesus as our Saviour from sin. Ask Him to give you His love for *everyone.*

(Place disciples, 2C-100)

The disciples needed to learn to love people different from themselves. They really did not understand the Son of God and His concern for the Samaritan woman and the people she would tell of Him. He was looking away to the city into which the woman had disappeared. He did not want to eat the food they brought. "It is more important to finish the work God has for me to do than to eat," He said.

Scene 7 (outdoor)

(Place woman, 2C-105 and Samaritan men, 2C-108 and 2C-109)

The disciples looked, too. The woman was coming back, bringing other Samaritans with her. The disciples listened as they explained their reason for coming. "We never saw such an excited woman. She said she had met the Christ. She insisted we come and meet Him, too."

We do not know all that happened when these people met the Lord and His disciples. But, we do know the Samaritans invited the Lord Jesus and His disciples to the city and they went.

(Remove figures)

Scene 8 (street scene)

(Place figures 2C-100, 105, 108-110, disciples, Samaritans and Christ)

The disciples were always learning new things from the Lord Jesus. Now, they knew He loved and accepted Samaritans. They stayed in the city for several days. Many other Samaritans beside the woman believed in the Lord Jesus Christ.

"We believed at first because of you," they said to the woman, "but now we believe because we have heard Him for ourselves. We know that this is indeed the Christ, the Saviour of the *world* (John 4:42). The disciples understood that the *world* included the Samaritans.

It is easy to say that you know the Lord Jesus came for the world. But, do you really act as though you believe it? Do you let Him use you to show His love and concern to those who are different from yourself? You can invite them to COME and receive the Lord Jesus Christ. They probably will not listen to you until you can show them that you love them, and truly care about them. Trust the Lord Jesus to give you His love for everyone.

How can you show your love and concern to those who are in some ways different from you? (Initiate discussion. The person may be lame or of another color or not have nice things. They might be old and not have friends. They may be rude or unkind. Teacher, guide the children in making positive suggestions of ways they can help. Kindness, patience, involvement, invitation to "Come" to Christ or club or both, etc.) Try to show love to some person this week and be ready to tell us about it. Perhaps you can even bring that person with you to club next week!

(Close in prayer asking His help in this. Remind children, who desire to receive Christ, of a place to meet you for further help.)

LESSON TEN

MIRACLE WORKER— RECEIVED AND REJECTED
(Healing Of Nobleman's Son, Rejection at Nazareth)

Scripture
John 4:45-54; Luke 4:16-32

Aim
That seeing the contrast between receiving and refusing Christ, the child may choose to receive Him and trust Him to help in time of need.

Memory Verse
John 1:11,12 — "He came unto his own, and his own received him not. But as many as received him, to them gave he power to become the sons of God, even to them that believe on his name."

Teaching the Memory Verse
We've learned that God the Son, the Lord Jesus Christ, worked with God the Father and the Holy Spirit in creating this world and everything in it. Then, one day He came from Heaven as a tiny baby to the world that He had made. He grew to be a man and began His work on earth. His own people did not want Him. They refused Him, or "received Him not." They said "no" to the Lord Jesus.

But even though most of them said "no," there were some who said "yes." They received Him. What did He do for them? Made them children of God! The word "power" in our verse means "the right." We could read it like this: But as many as received him to them he gave the right to become the *children* of God . . .

When we believe what He did for us and receive Him we are born into the family of God. There is a "forever difference" in the lives of those who *refuse* or *receive*. (Show wordstrips.) We'll learn more about it in our lesson. (Drill verse by quoting verse 11 and singing verse 12. See suggested songs.)

Review Questions
Let's think about our last lesson where someone received the Lord Jesus.

1. At the time when our lessons took place, the Jews who lived in Galilee and Judea did not love the people of Samaria. (Show map from last week.) In what one way did they show this?
A. They did not travel through the country of Samaria.
2. How did the Lord Jesus feel about the people of Samaria?
A. He loved them.
3. What did He do that showed that He loved them?
A. He traveled through their country.
4. What other thing did He do which seemed strange to His disciples?
A. He talked with a Samaritan woman at the well.
5. What did Jesus ask her to do?
A. "Give me a drink"
6. Why was she surprised at His request?
A. She did not expect Him to speak to her because He was a Jew.
7. What did Jesus say He could give her?
A. Living water.
8. Can you explain "living water"?
(Teacher: This is a hard question and you may need to help with the answer.)
A. As water satisfies the need of your body when you are thirsty, Jesus can satisfy the real you, because He can forgive your sin. (If it is necessary to clarify "the real you" again, be sure to do so.)
9. What new lesson did the disciples learn from the Lord Jesus at this time?
A. That He loved and accepted anyone. He loves all kinds of people.

10. What lessons can you learn through what Jesus did that day?
A. (Give opportunity for various answers here, but, be sure to include our love and concern for those who are different from ourselves. Discuss ways the children have done this since the last lesson.)

Suggested Alternate Review
A different way to review this lesson could be a role play situation. Assign early arrivals to be disciples, Samaritan woman and men from the city. Place labels on each for identification. Assign a child to act as a reporter. He questions the others as to what took place at the well and in the city of Sychar. Teacher will need to guide to bring out meaningful answers.

Suggested Songs
Salvation Songs Number 1: "Come to the Saviour," No. 21 (verse 1 only); "There's Nothing Too Hard for Thee," No. 65
Salvation Songs Number 2: "The Gospel," No. 95; "Just Like Nicodemus," No. 92; "Jesus Gave Her Water," No. 91; "John 1:12," No. 79
Salvation Songs Number 4: "I Have Decided to Follow Jesus," No. 76

Schedule For Teaching
Song — "Come to the Saviour" (verse 1 only) — Discuss the way and who found the way — Nicodemus and Samaritan woman — introducing during next songs.
Song — "Jesus Gave Her Water"
Song — "Just Like Nicodemus"
Song — "I Have Decided to Follow Jesus"
Teach Memory Verse — John 1:11,12
Song — "John 1:12"
Review Questions
Song — "The Gospel"
Lesson — "Miracle Worker — Received and Rejected"
Song — "There's Nothing Too Hard for Thee"
Application of Truth

Visual Aids
Use plain flannelboard; outdoor and indoor and temple scenes; two booklets for opening illustrations; figures 2C-111 — 2C-127; Tape figure 2C-115 to right side of figure 2C-114, folding over to complete scene as you speak of the servant coming to nobleman.
Print wordstrips *refuse* and *receive* for use in memory verse and lesson application.

Lesson
I am going to give you a word and you give me the opposite word. Come (go). Walk (run). Hurry (wait). Work (play). Noise (silence). No (yes). There is no end to opposites. Maybe you would like to give me some. Now, can you give me the opposite words in the meaning of our verse today? Refuse and receive. Let's make sure we understand those words. (Teacher: Write "refuse" and "receive" on chalkboard or place at top of flannelboard. Have a plan similar to the following *arranged* between you and two of your students to strengthen this thought).
Teacher: I have a booklet here for each of you, Ray and Gail. (Offer each some small book. A copy of DAILY BREAD FOR GIRLS AND BOYS is excellent) This has a page to read for each day of the month. It has something for you to read from God's Word each day and story for each day.
Gail: Oh, thank you. I'm sure I'll like it.
Ray: No, thanks. I'd rather not have the book.
Teacher: Why don't you want it, Ray?
Ray: If I took it I'd feel as if I had to read it every day and I'm not sure I want to do that.

Teacher to students: What did Gail do? What did Ray do? (See that the words "receive" and "refuse" are used. Draw attention to wordstrips again.) Thank you Ray and Gail. Ray is not really saying "no" to reading God's Word. We planned to do this so that you would understand "refuse" and "receive" better.

Scene 1 (plain board)
(Place figure of Christ, 2C-111)
During two wonderful days in Samaria many people there received the Lord Jesus Christ. After that He went back to His home country, Galilee.
It seems the Lord Jesus may have been surprised at the welcome home the Galileans gave Him (cf. John 4:43-45). Many of the people from Galilee were in Jerusalem when the Lord Jesus was there. They saw Him make the buyers and sellers leave the temple. They had also seen Him do miracles in Jerusalem. Now they were eager to see what He would do in Galilee. But, He did not call the crowd together and do some great miracle. Instead, He just went quietly to the little village of Cana. Perhaps He went home with His disciple, Nathaniel.
(Remove figure)

Scene 2 (plain board)
(Place nobleman, figure 2C-112)
At that very time a worried man was on his way to Cana. He was coming from Capernaum, a city about 20 miles away. Even though he hurried toward Cana he was thinking about home.
(Hold figure 2C-113 in hands, showing nobleman's thoughts)

A very sick little boy was back home in Capernaum.
The man probably remembered things as they happened. His wife had been so upset when she told him, "Our little son has a very high fever."
"We will get the best doctor," the nobleman had replied.
They could get the very best doctor. They had plenty of money. The man was an officer of the king. But, the medicine of the best doctor did not help.
(Lay aside 2C-113; hold 2C-114)
The boy kept getting worse. Finally even the doctor had said, "I cannot do any more to help him."
The officer and his wife knew that money could not buy health for their son. Was there nothing more to do? All hope seemed to be gone.
(Fold over 2C-115, messenger)
Then, someone reported, "Jesus is in Cana."
Jesus? Ah, yes! The one who turned the water into wine. Would He come and heal their son?
(Lay aside figure 2C-114 and 2C-115)
Early in the morning the man had started on his way to

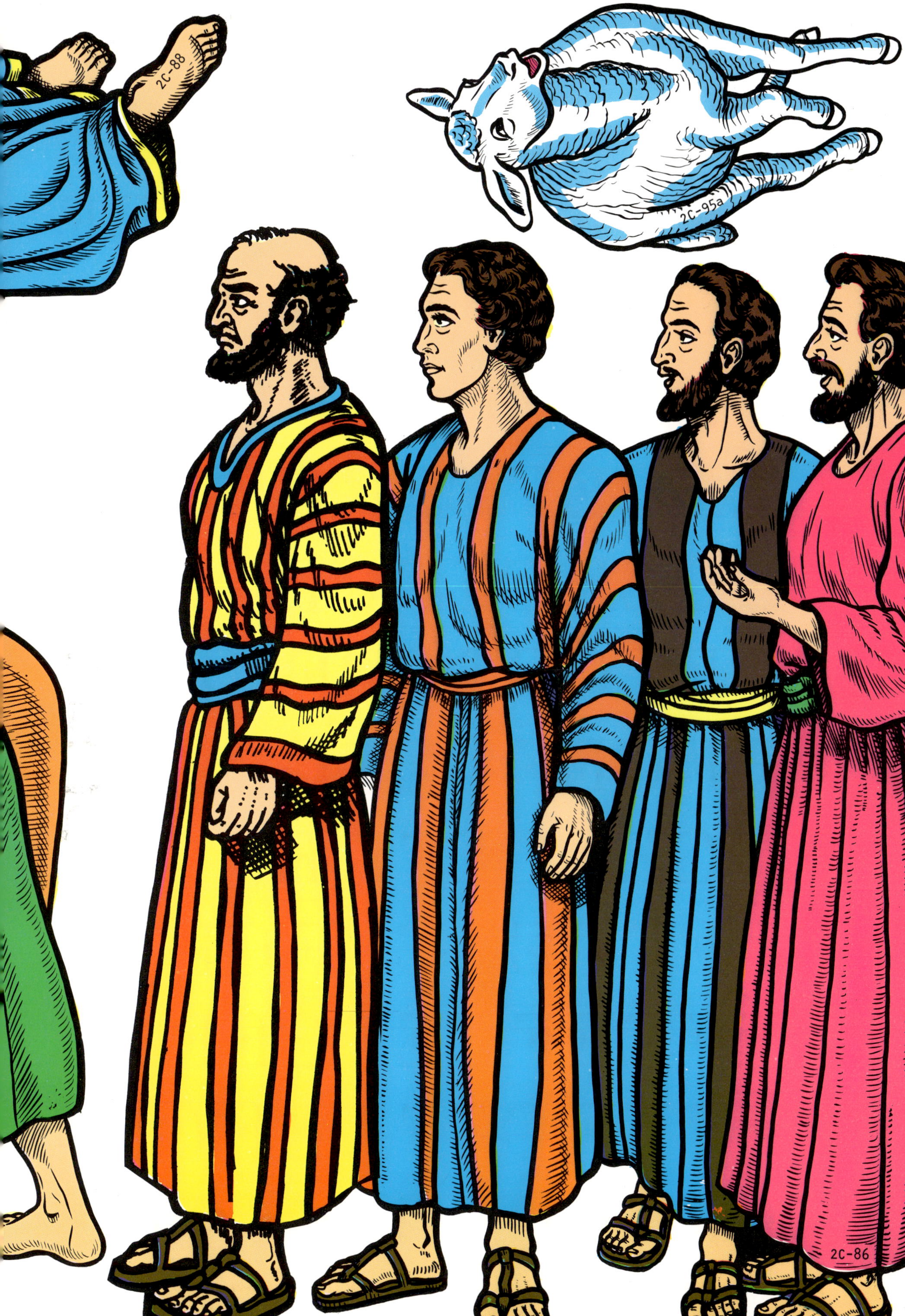
2C-88
2C-95a
2C-86

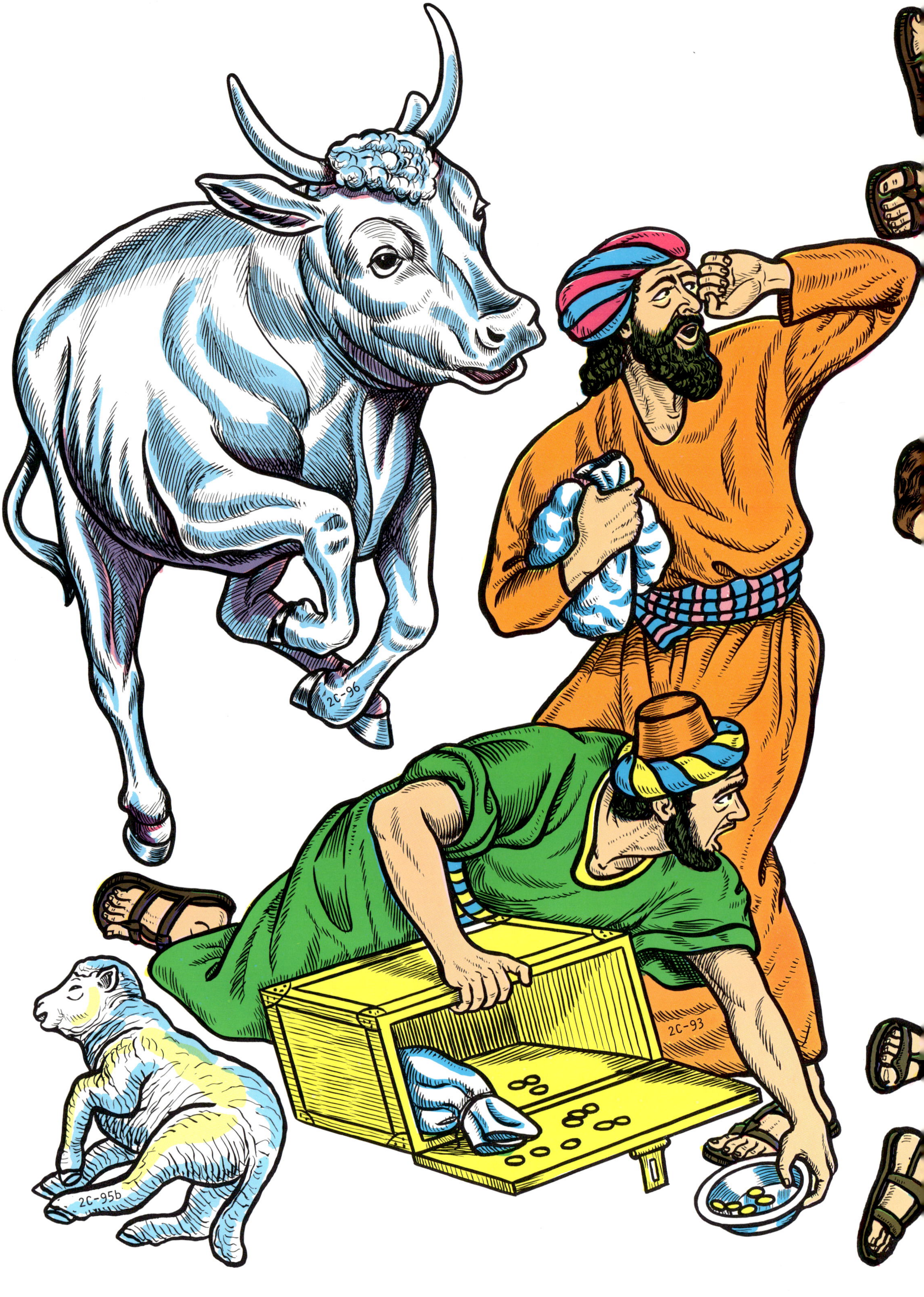
2C-96
2C-93
2C-95b

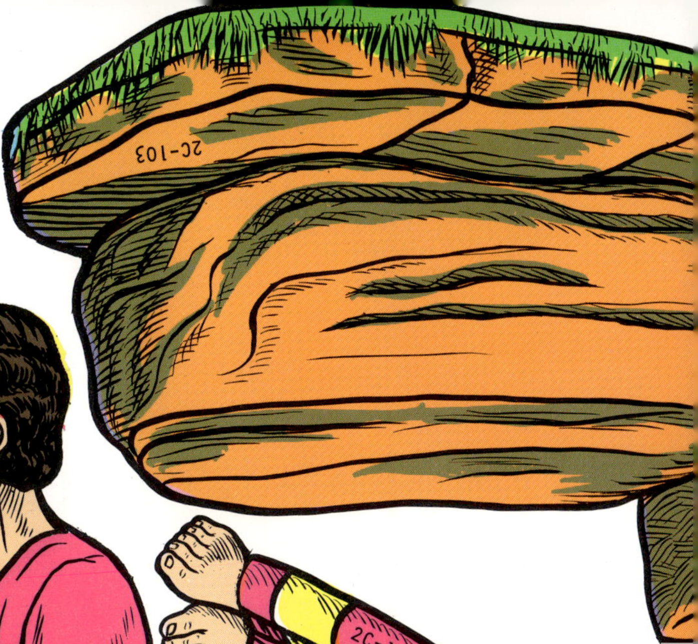
2C-103

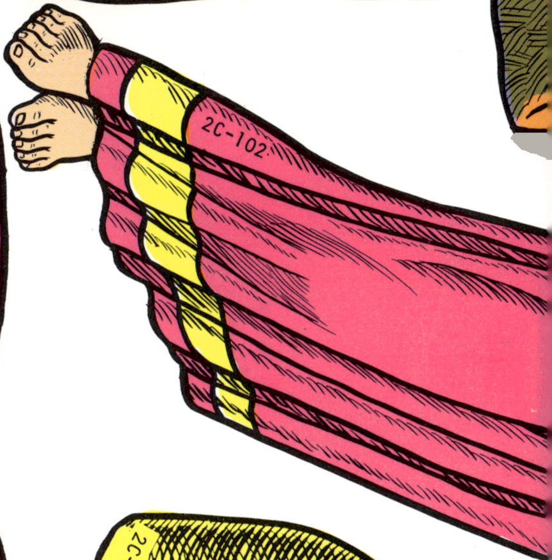
2C-102

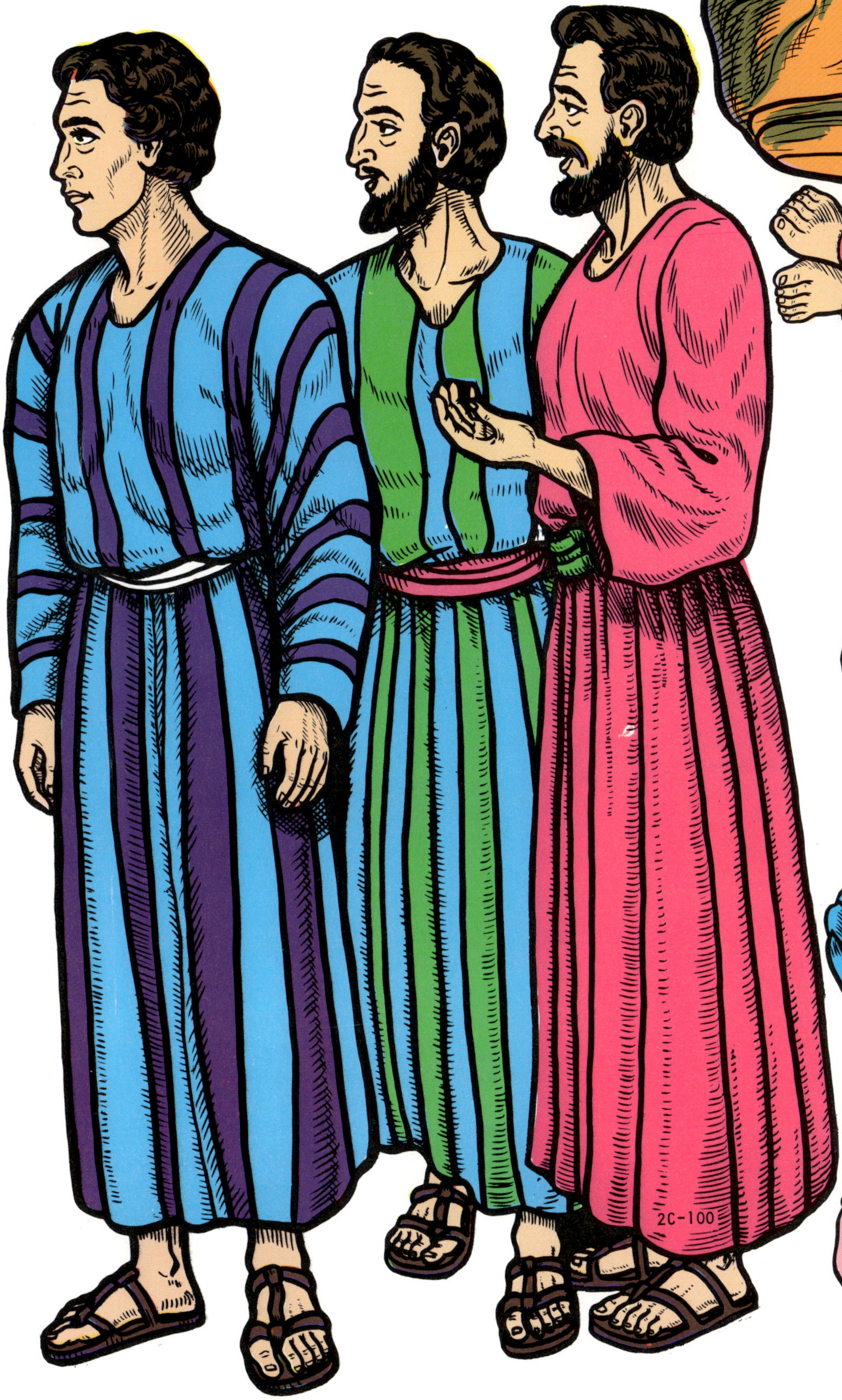
2C-100

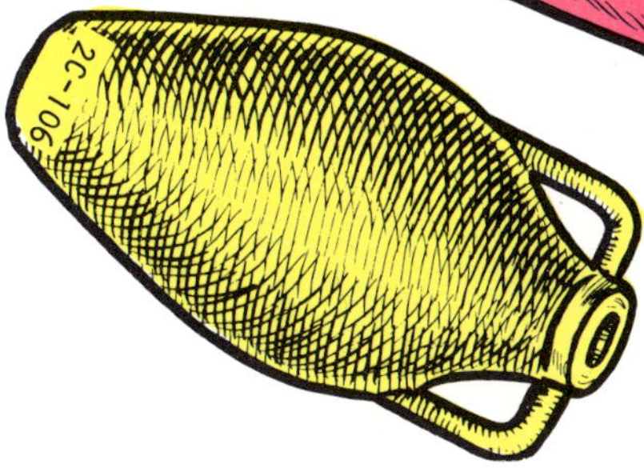
2C-106

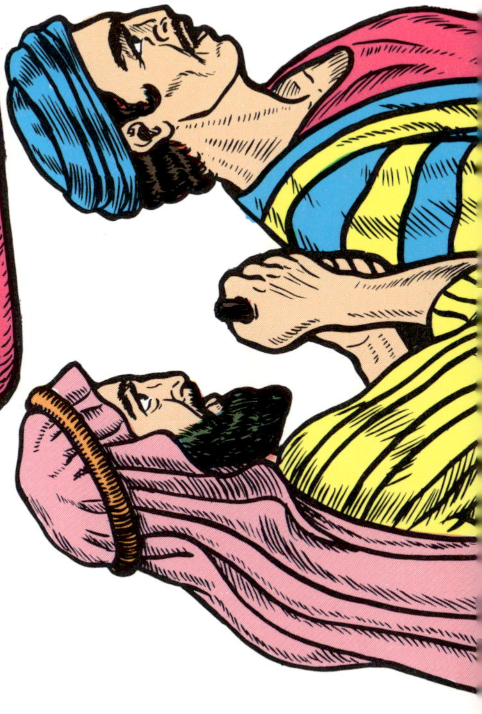

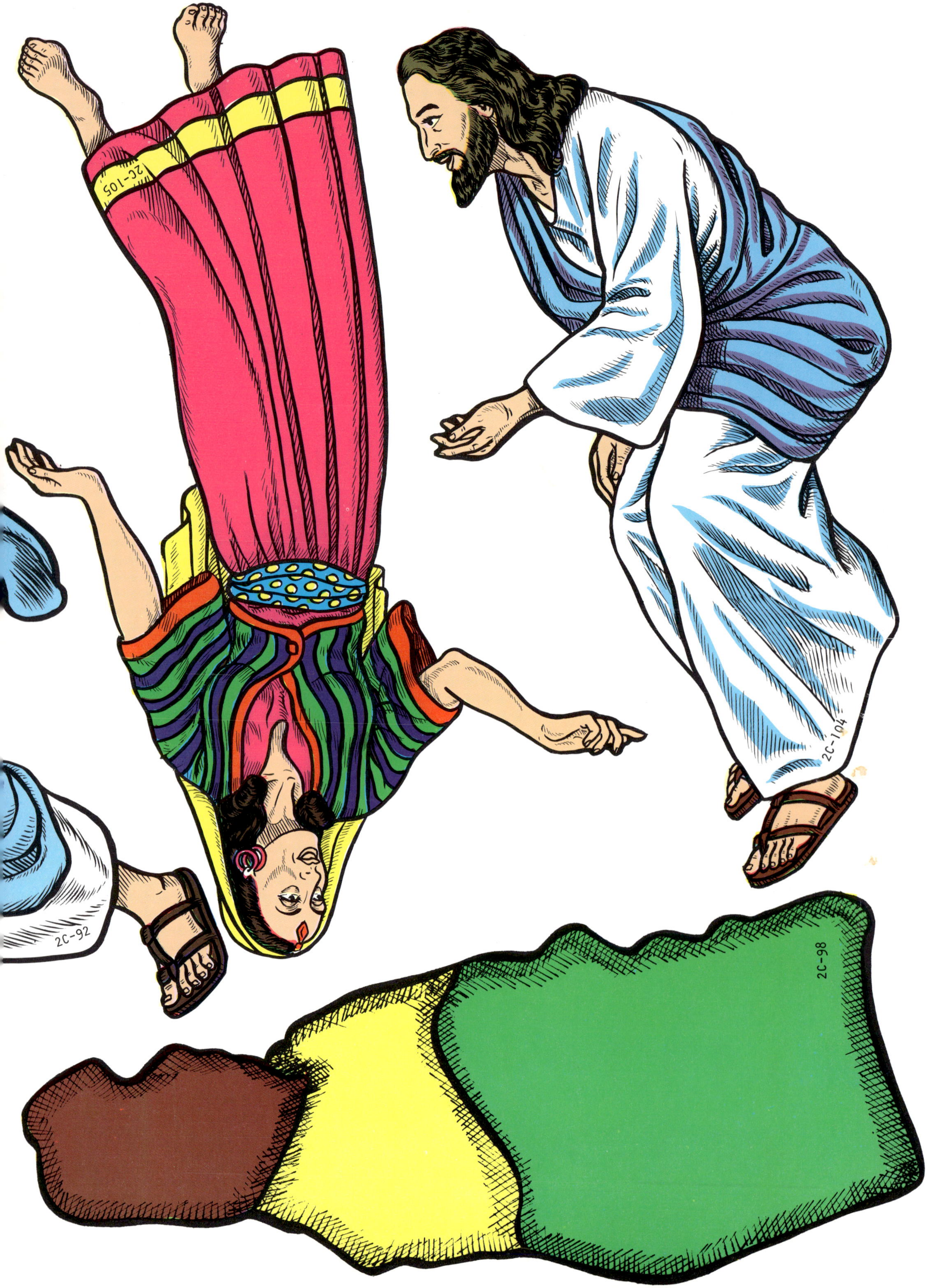
2C-105
2C-104
2C-92
2C-98

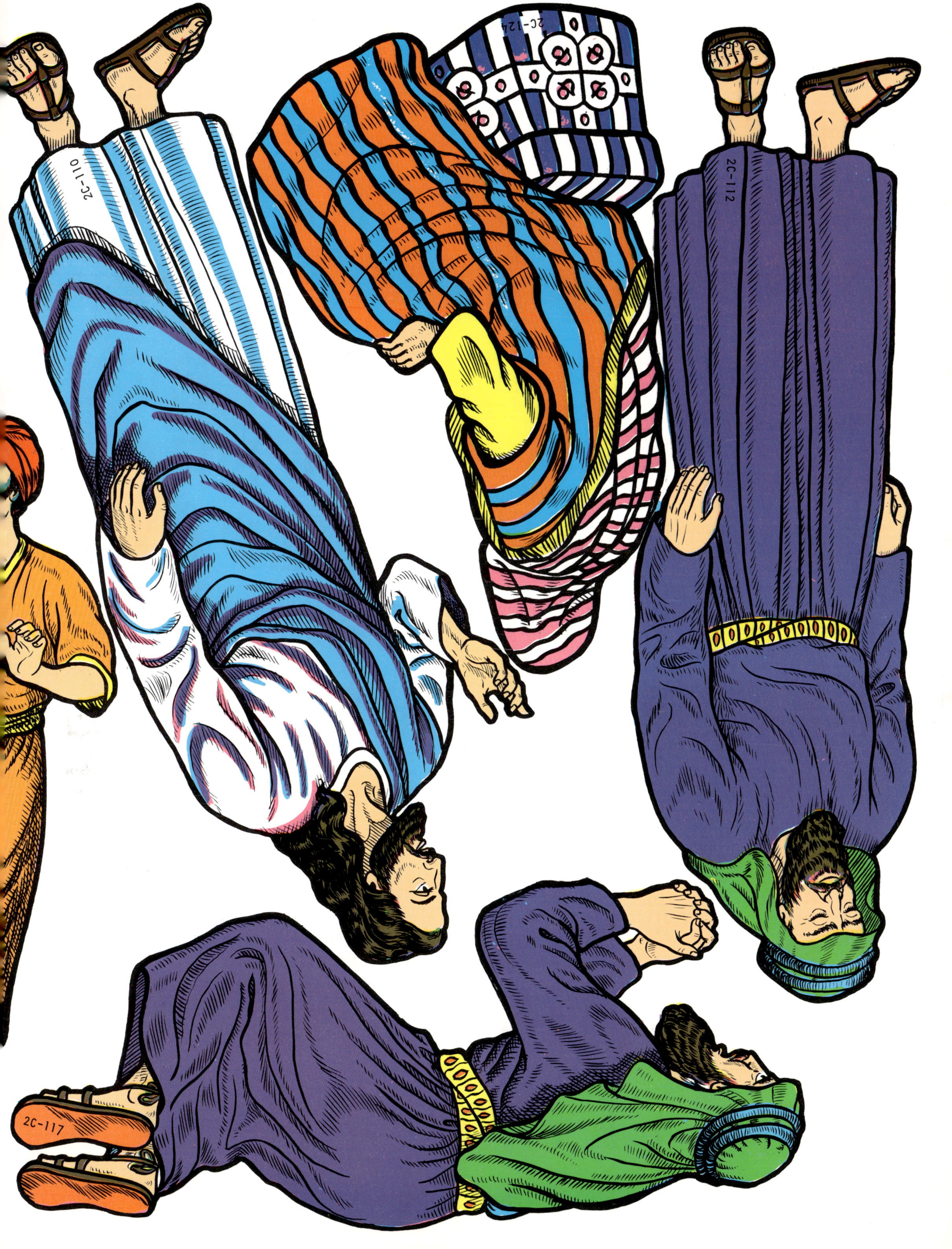
2C-110
2C-124
2C-112
2C-117

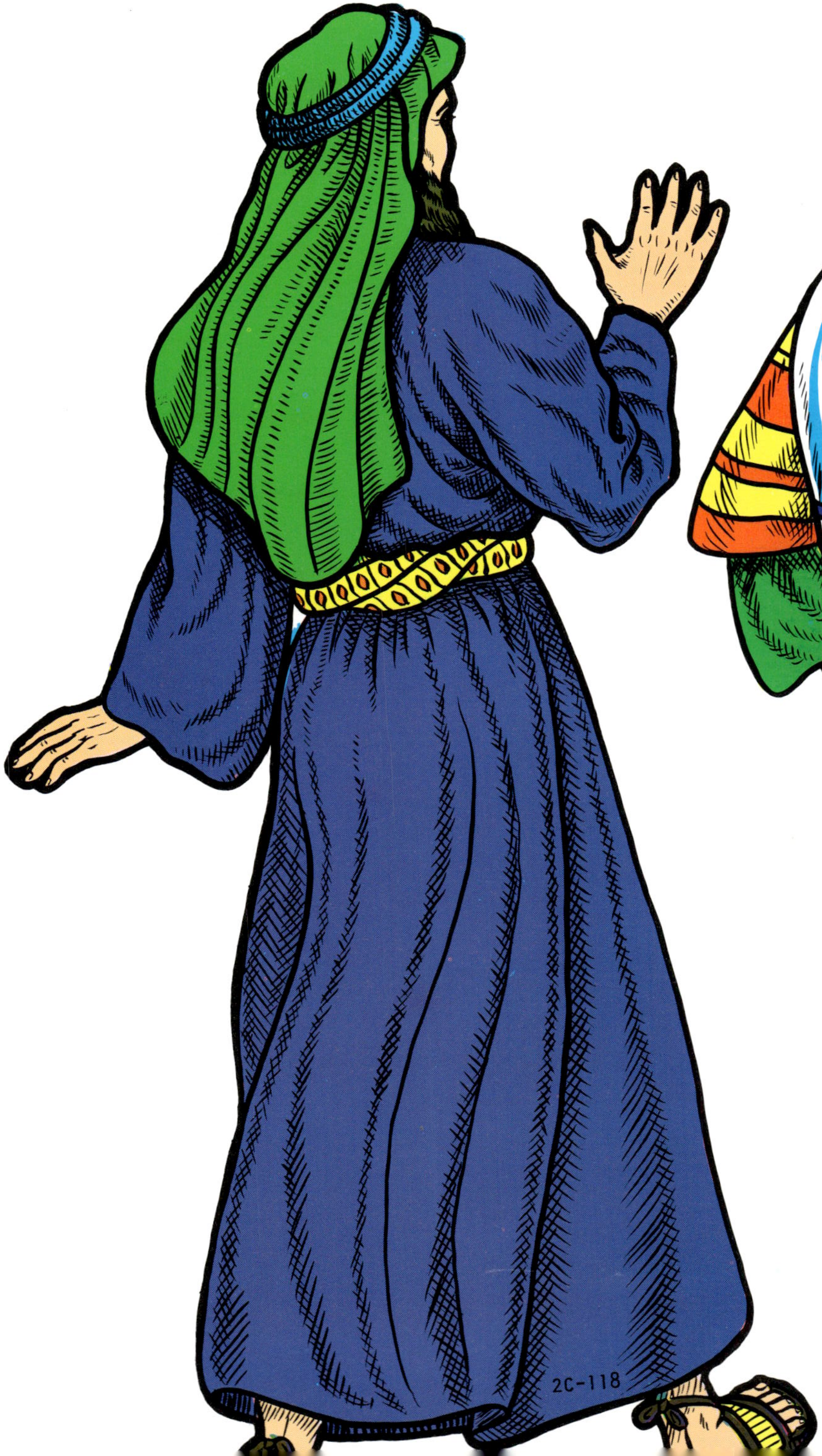
2C-118

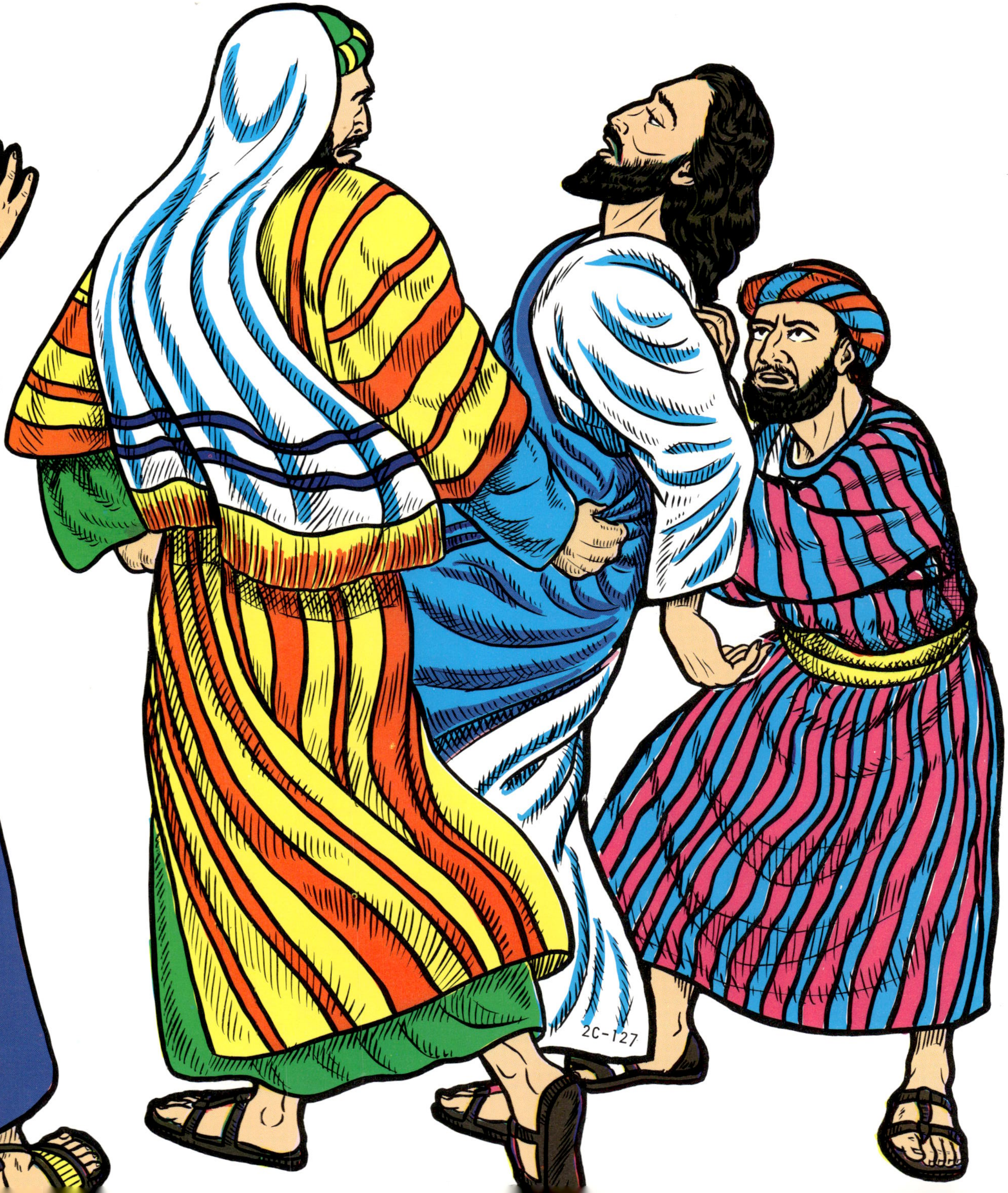
2C-127

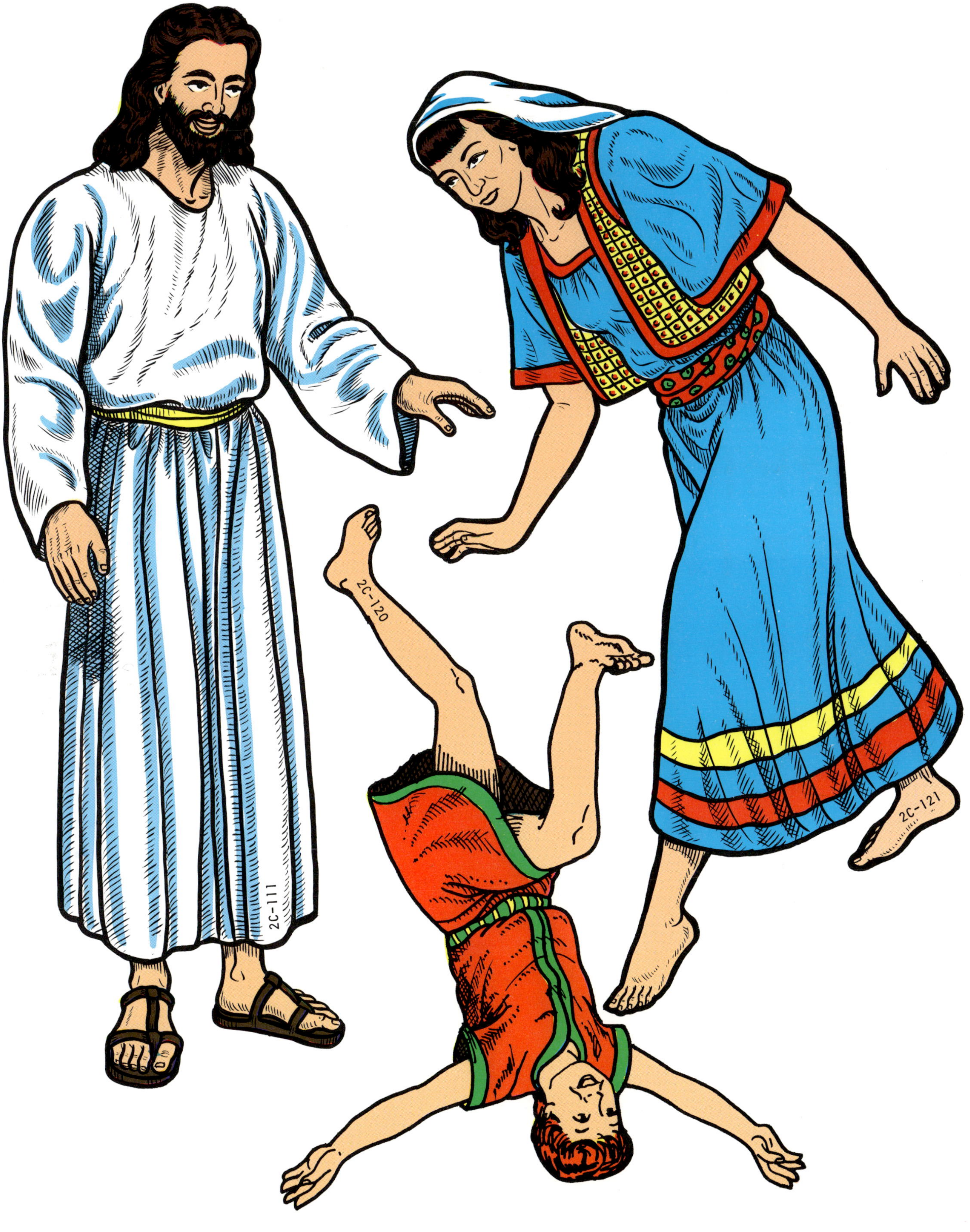
2C-111
2C-120
2C-121

CEF CEF CEF CEF CEF CEF
EF CEF CEF CEF CEF CEF CEF
F CEF CEF CEF CEF CEF C
CEF CEF CEF CEF CEF CE
EF CEF CEF CEF CEF CEF C
F CEF CEF CEF CEF CEF C
CEF CEF CEF CEF CEF CE
EF CEF CEF CEF CEF CEF
F CEF CEF CEF CEF CEF C
CEF CEF CEF CEF CEF C
EF CEF CEF CEF CEF CEF
F CEF CEF CEF CEF CEF C
CEF CEF CEF CEF CEF CI
EF CEF CEF CEF CEF CEF
F CEF CEF CEF CEF CEF C

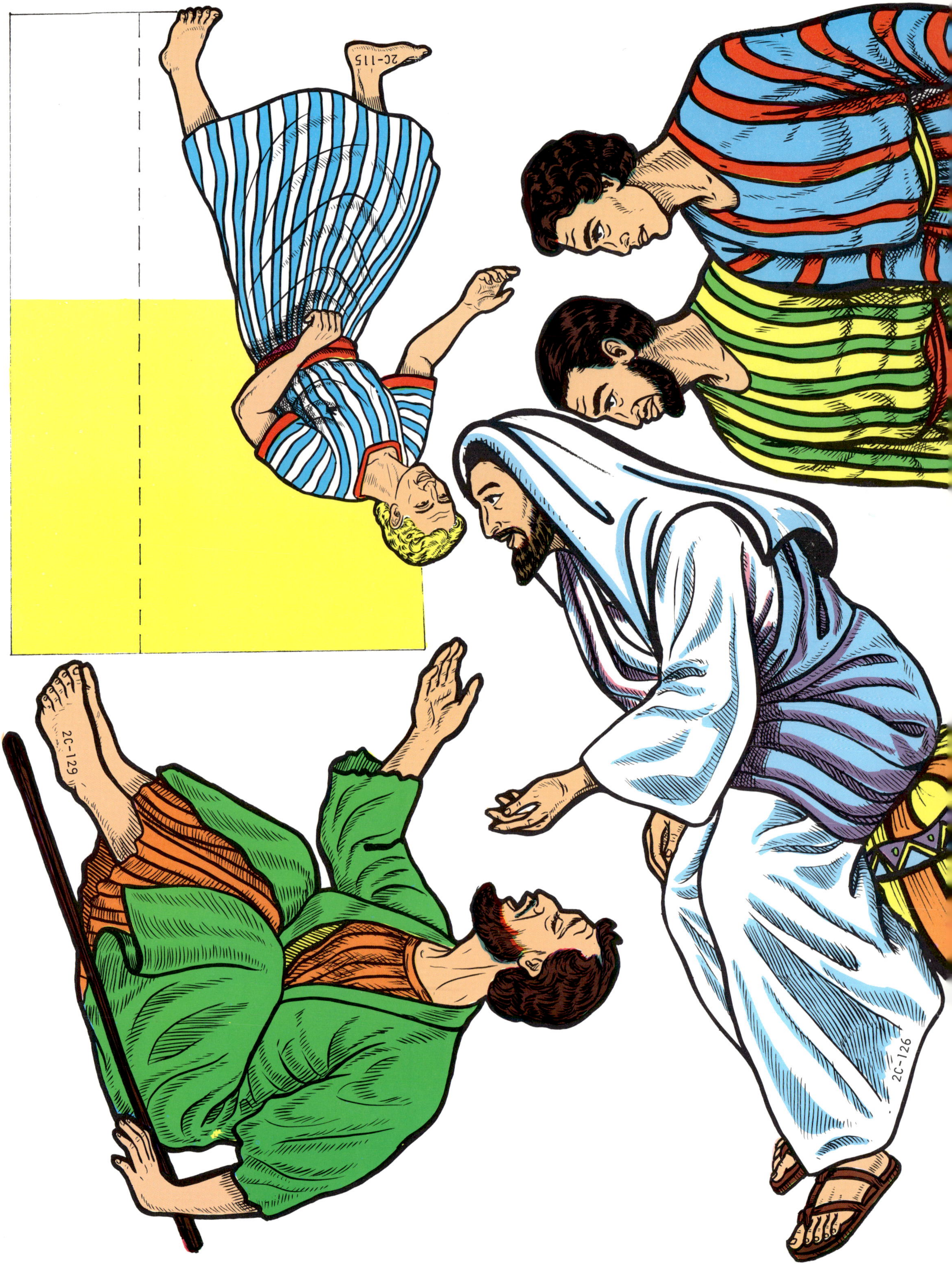
2C-129
2C-126
2C-115

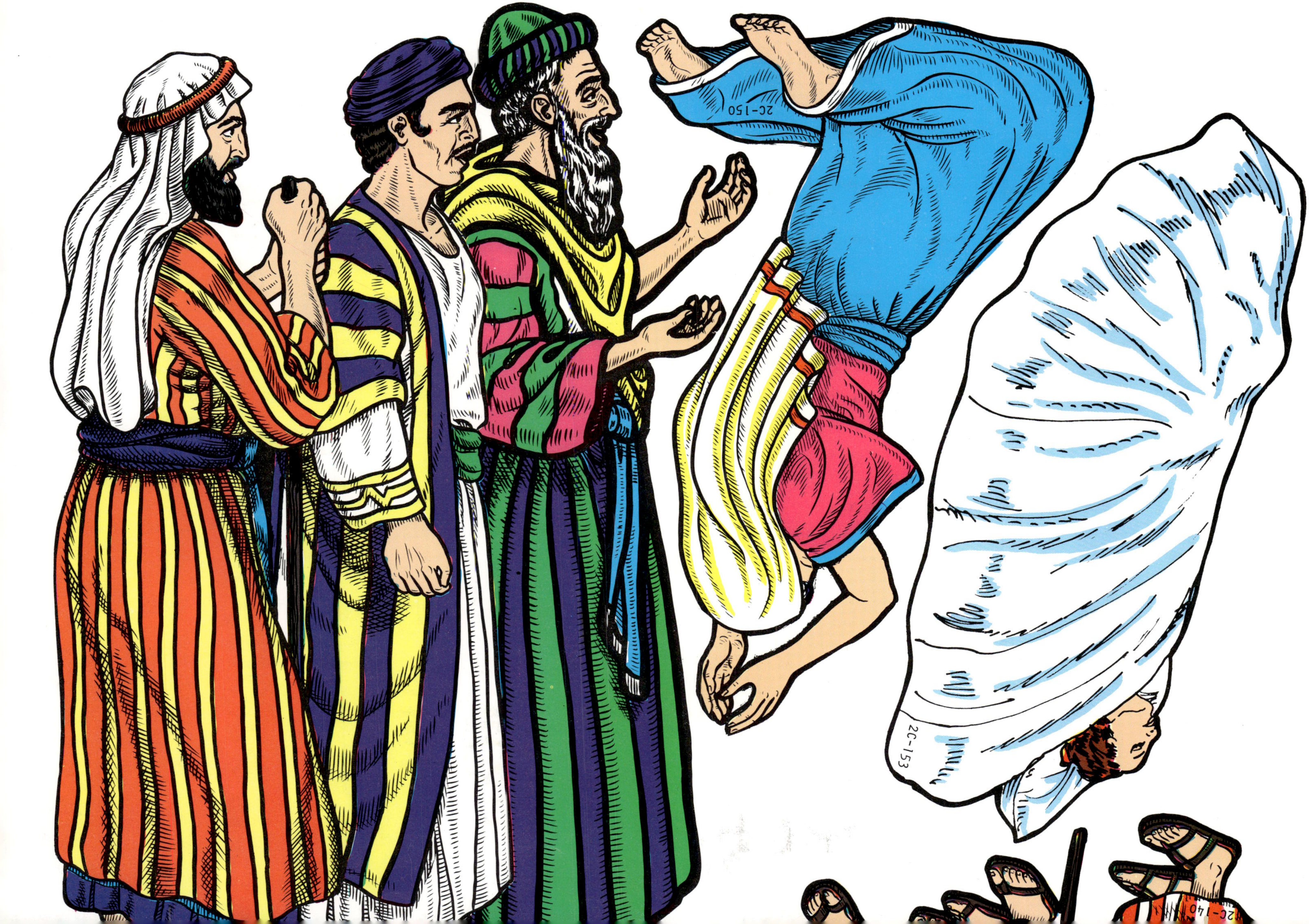
2C-150
2C-153

EF CEF CEF CEF CEF CEF
F CEF CEF CEF CEF CEF C
CEF CEF CEF CEF CEF CE
EF CEF CEF CEF CEF CEF
F CEF CEF CEF CEF CEF C
CEF CEF CEF CEF CEF CE
EF CEF CEF CEF CEF CEF
F CEF CEF CEF CEF CEF C
CEF CEF CEF CEF CEF CE
EF CEF CEF CEF CEF CEF
F CEF CEF CEF CEF CEF C
CEF CEF CEF CEF CEF CE
EF CEF CEF CEF CEF CEF
F CEF CEF CEF CEF CEF C
CEF CEF CEF CEF CEF CE

CEF CEF CEF CEF CEF CE
EF CEF CEF CEF CEF CEF
F CEF CEF CEF CEF CEF C
CEF CEF CEF CEF CEF CE
EF CEF CEF CEF CEF CEF
F CEF CEF CEF CEF CEF C
CEF CEF CEF CEF CEF CE
EF CEF CEF CEF CEF CEF
F CEF CEF CEF CEF CEF C
CEF CEF CEF CEF CEF CE
EF CEF CEF CEF CEF CEF
F CEF CEF CEF CEF CEF C
CEF CEF CEF CEF CEF CE
EF CEF CEF CEF CEF CEF
F CEF CEF CEF CEF CEF C

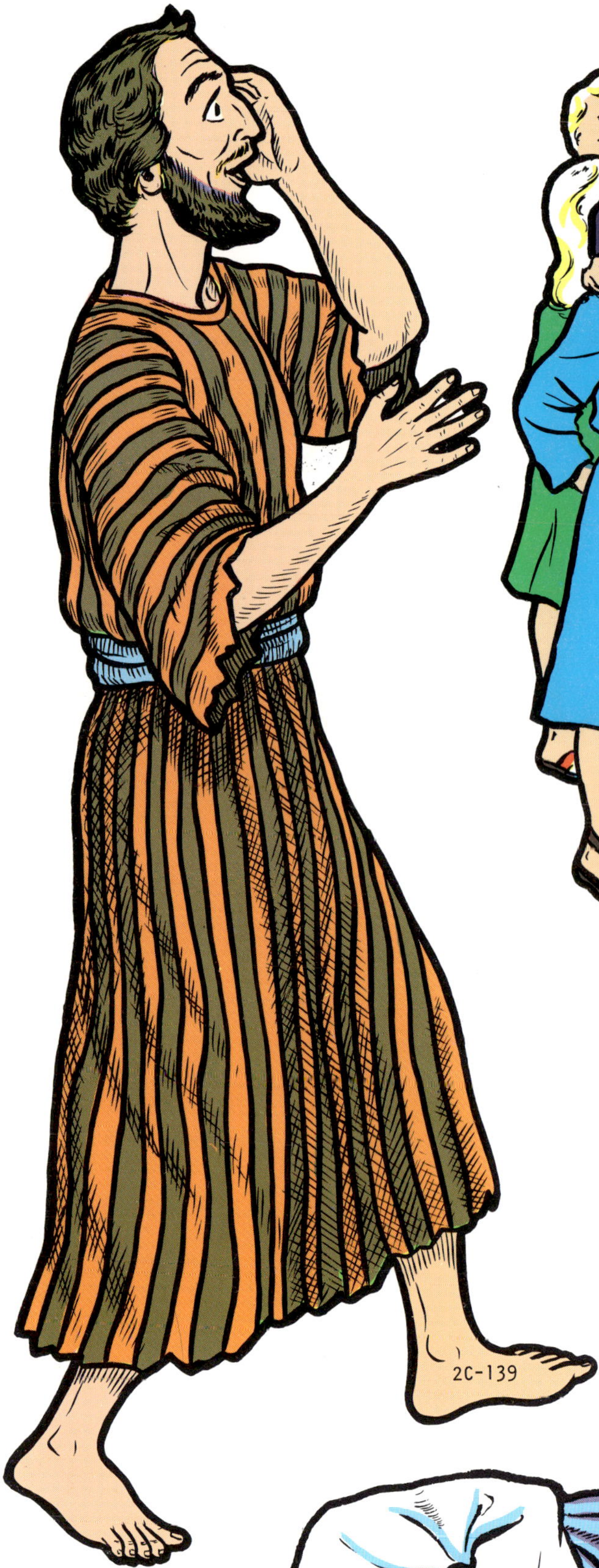
2C-139

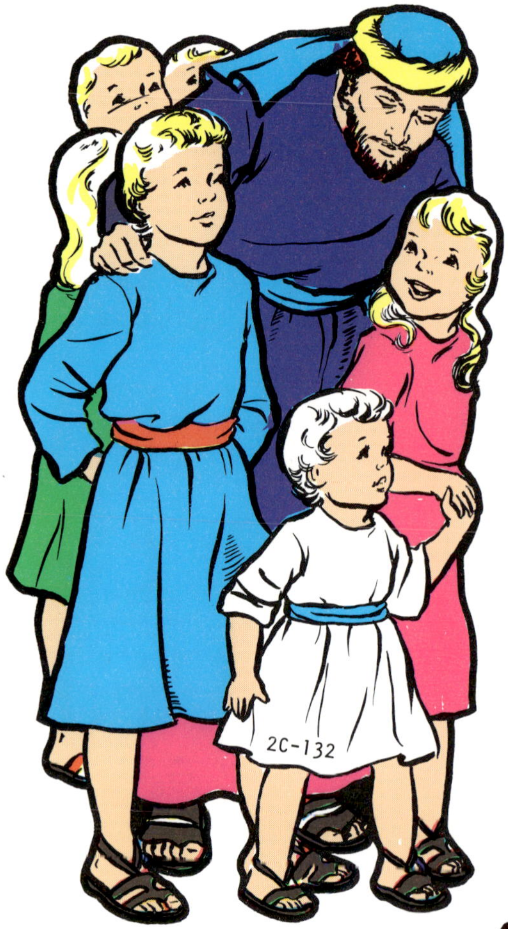
2C-132

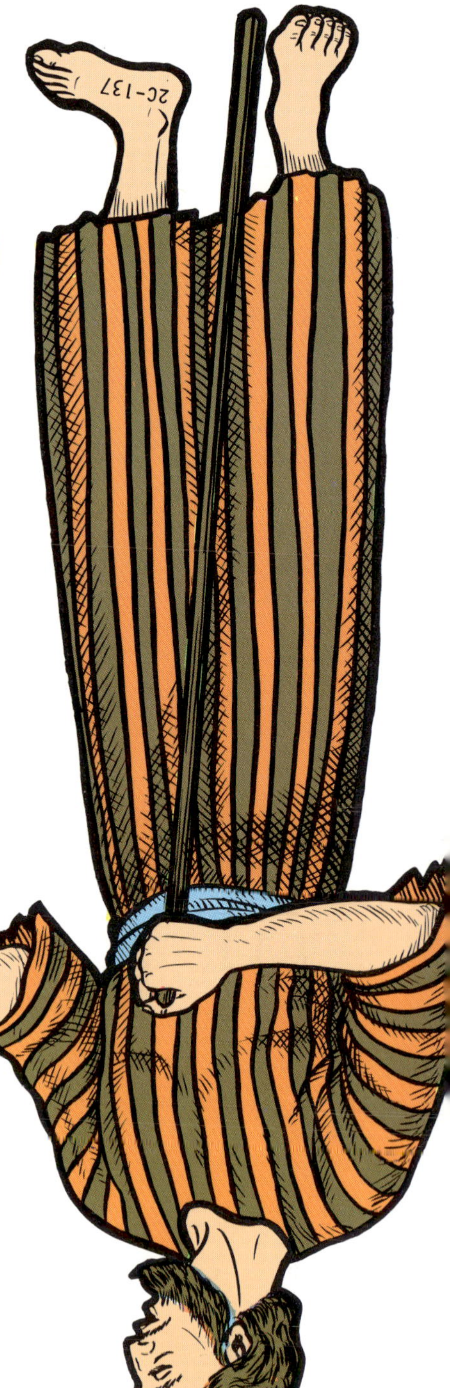
2C-137

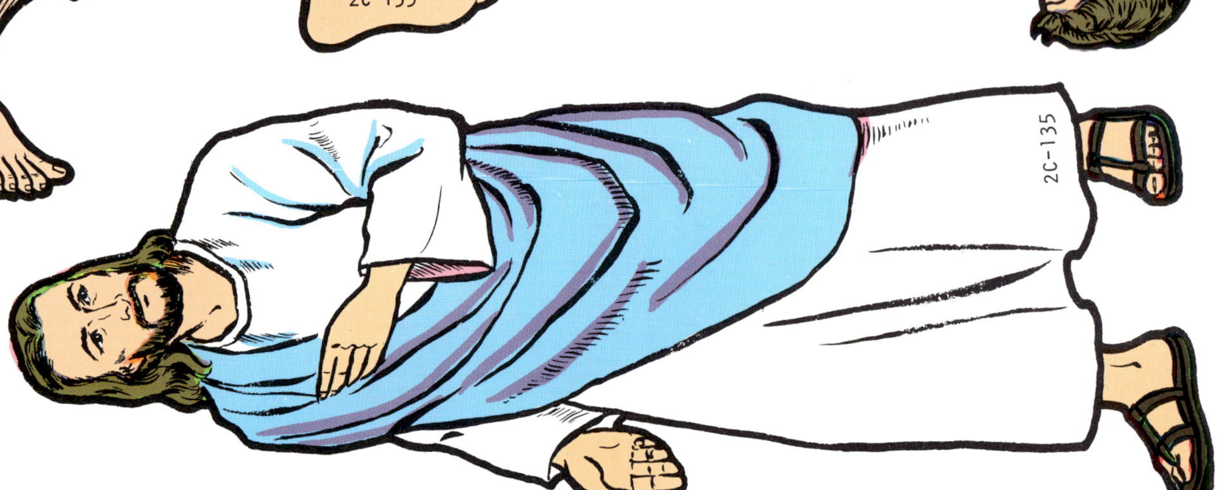
2C-135

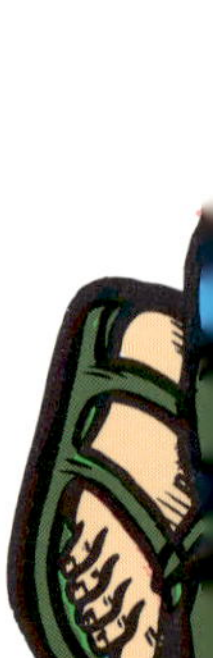

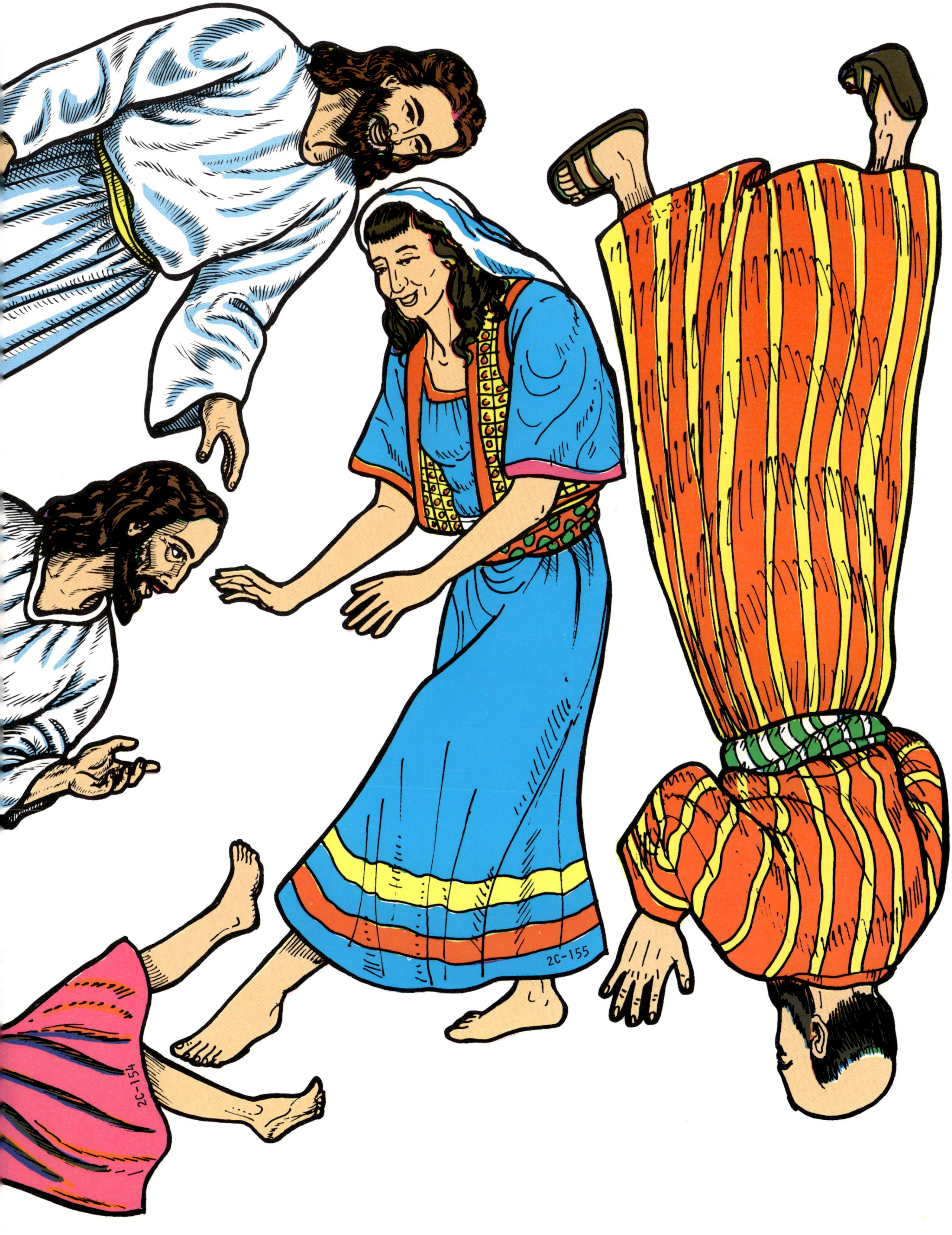
2C-151
2C-155
2C-154

EF CEF CEF CEF CEF CEF
F CEF CEF CEF CEF CEF C
CEF CEF CEF CEF CEF CE
EF CEF CEF CEF CEF CEF
F CEF CEF CEF CEF CEF C
CEF CEF CEF CEF CEF CE
EF CEF CEF CEF CEF CEF
F CEF CEF CEF CEF CEF C
CEF CEF CEF CEF CEF CE
EF CEF CEF CEF CEF CEF
F CEF CEF CEF CEF CEF C
CEF CEF CEF CEF CEF CE
EF CEF CEF CEF CEF CEF
F CEF CEF CEF CEF CEF C
CEF CEF CEF CEF CEF CE

CEF CEF CEF CEF CEF CEF
EF CEF CEF CEF CEF CEF
F CEF CEF CEF CEF CEF C
CEF CEF CEF CEF CEF CE
EF CEF CEF CEF CEF CEF
F CEF CEF CEF CEF CEF C
CEF CEF CEF CEF CEF CE
EF CEF CEF CEF CEF CEF
F CEF CEF CEF CEF CEF C
CEF CEF CEF CEF CEF CE
EF CEF CEF CEF CEF CEF
F CEF CEF CEF CEF CEF C
CEF CEF CEF CEF CEF CE
EF CEF CEF CEF CEF CEF
F CEF CEF CEF CEF CEF C

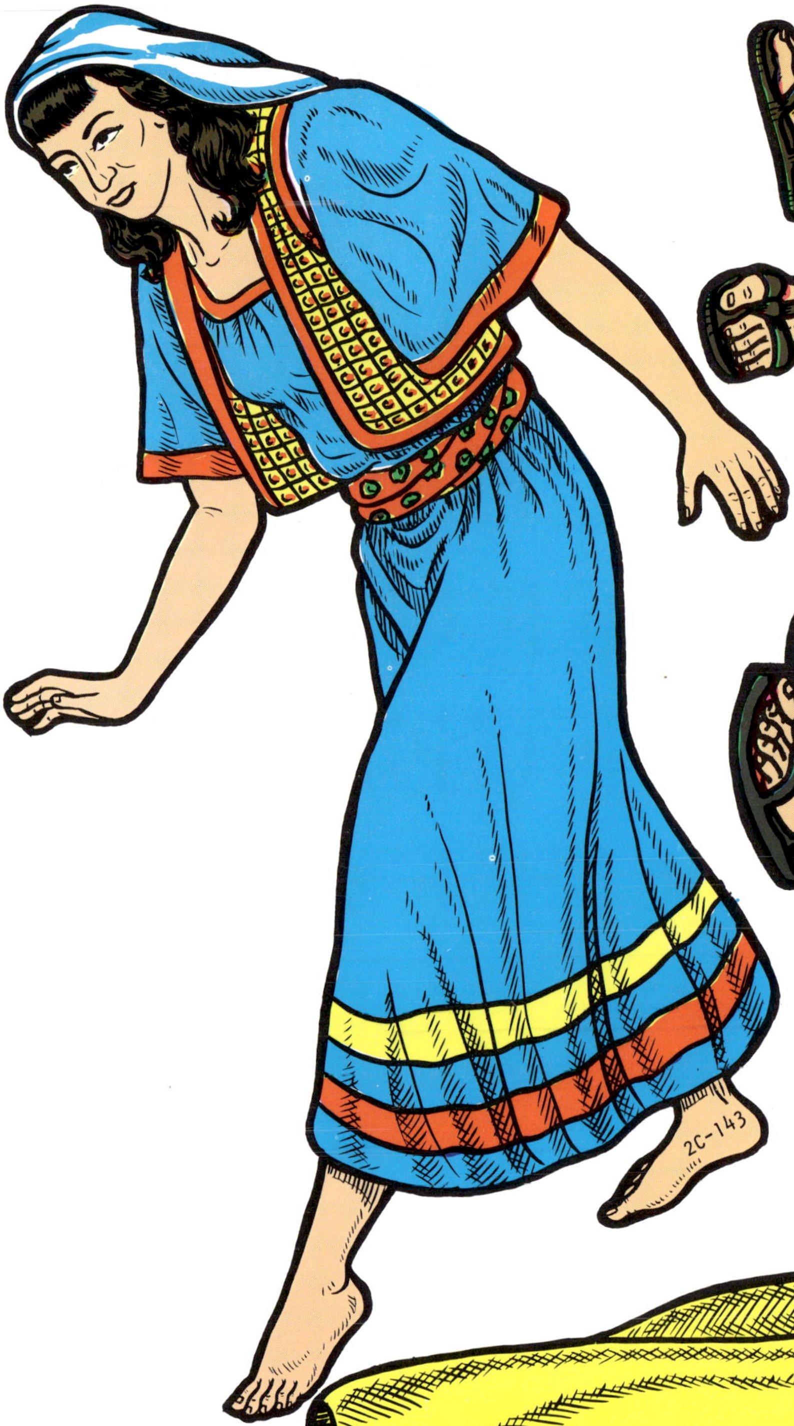
2C-143
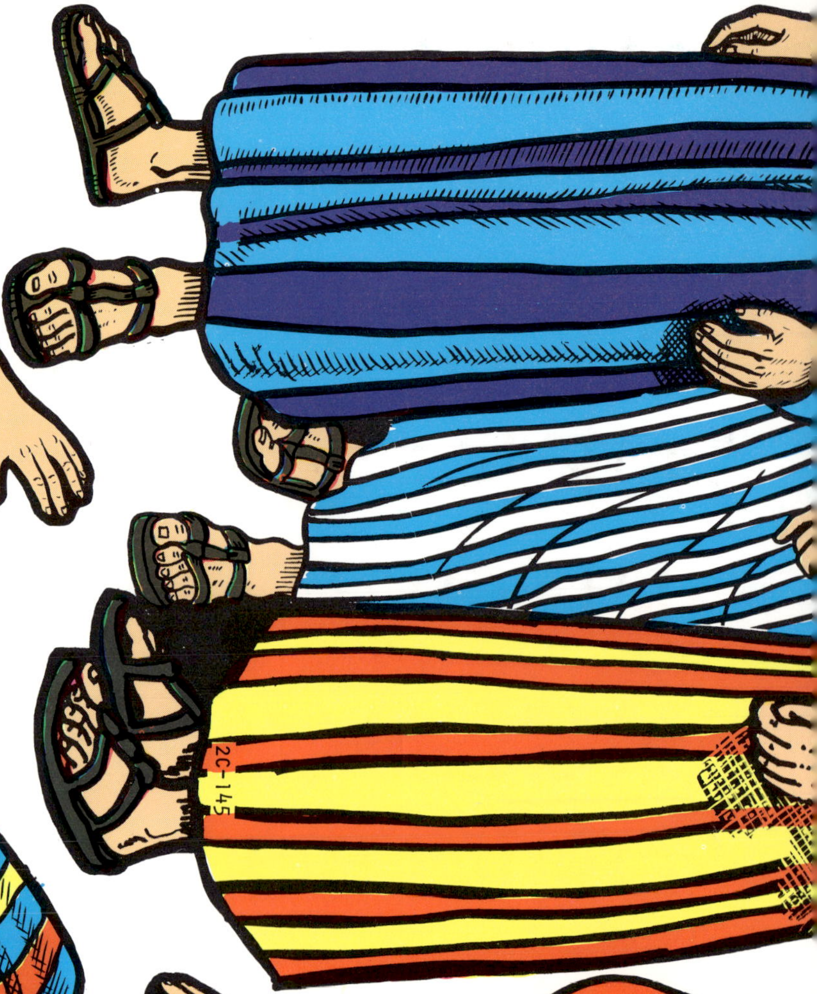
2C-145
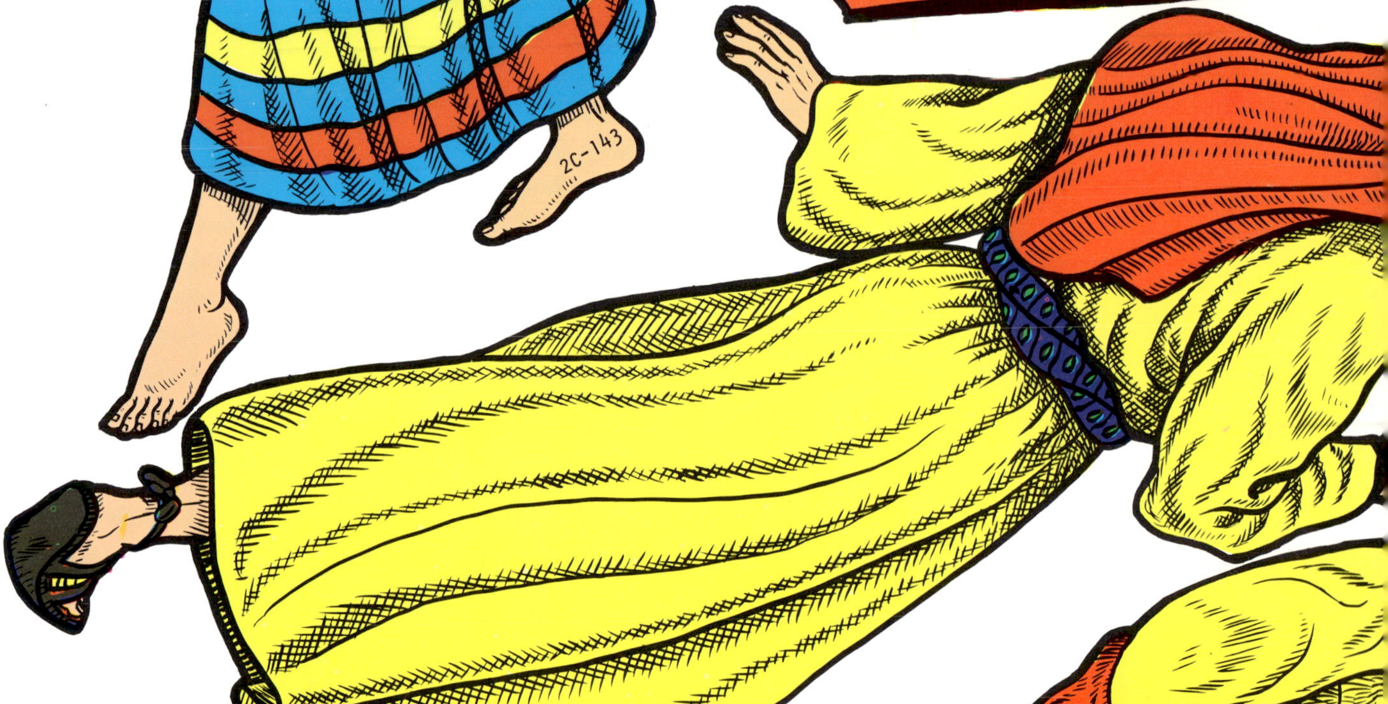
2C-146
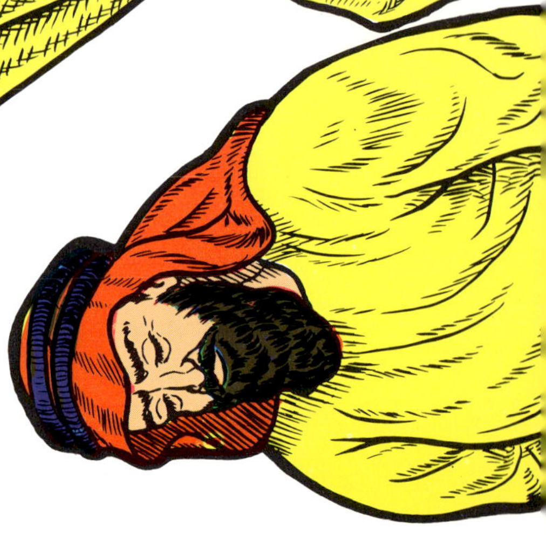

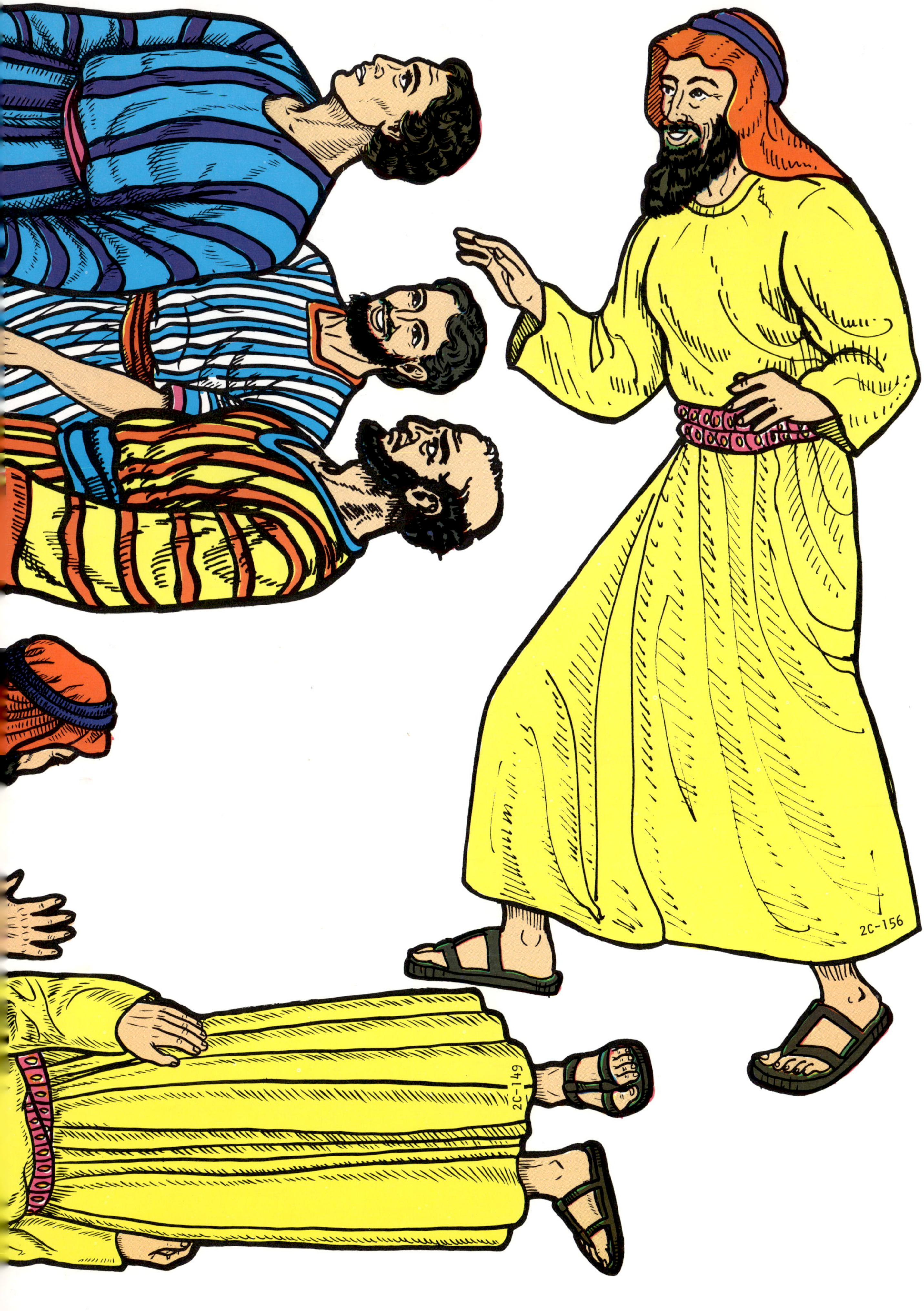
2C-156
2C-149

CEF CEF CEF CEF CEF CEF CEF
EF CEF CEF CEF CEF CEF CEF C
F CEF CEF CEF CEF CEF CEF CE
CEF CEF CEF CEF CEF CEF CEF
EF CEF CEF CEF CEF CEF CEF C
F CEF CEF CEF CEF CEF CEF CE
CEF CEF CEF CEF CEF CEF CEF
EF CEF CEF CEF CEF CEF CEF C
F CEF CEF CEF CEF CEF CEF CE
CEF CEF CEF CEF CEF CEF CEF
EF CEF CEF CEF CEF CEF CEF C
F CEF CEF CEF CEF CEF CEF CE
CEF CEF CEF CEF CEF CEF CEF
EF CEF CEF CEF CEF CEF CEF C
F CEF CEF CEF CEF CEF CEF CE

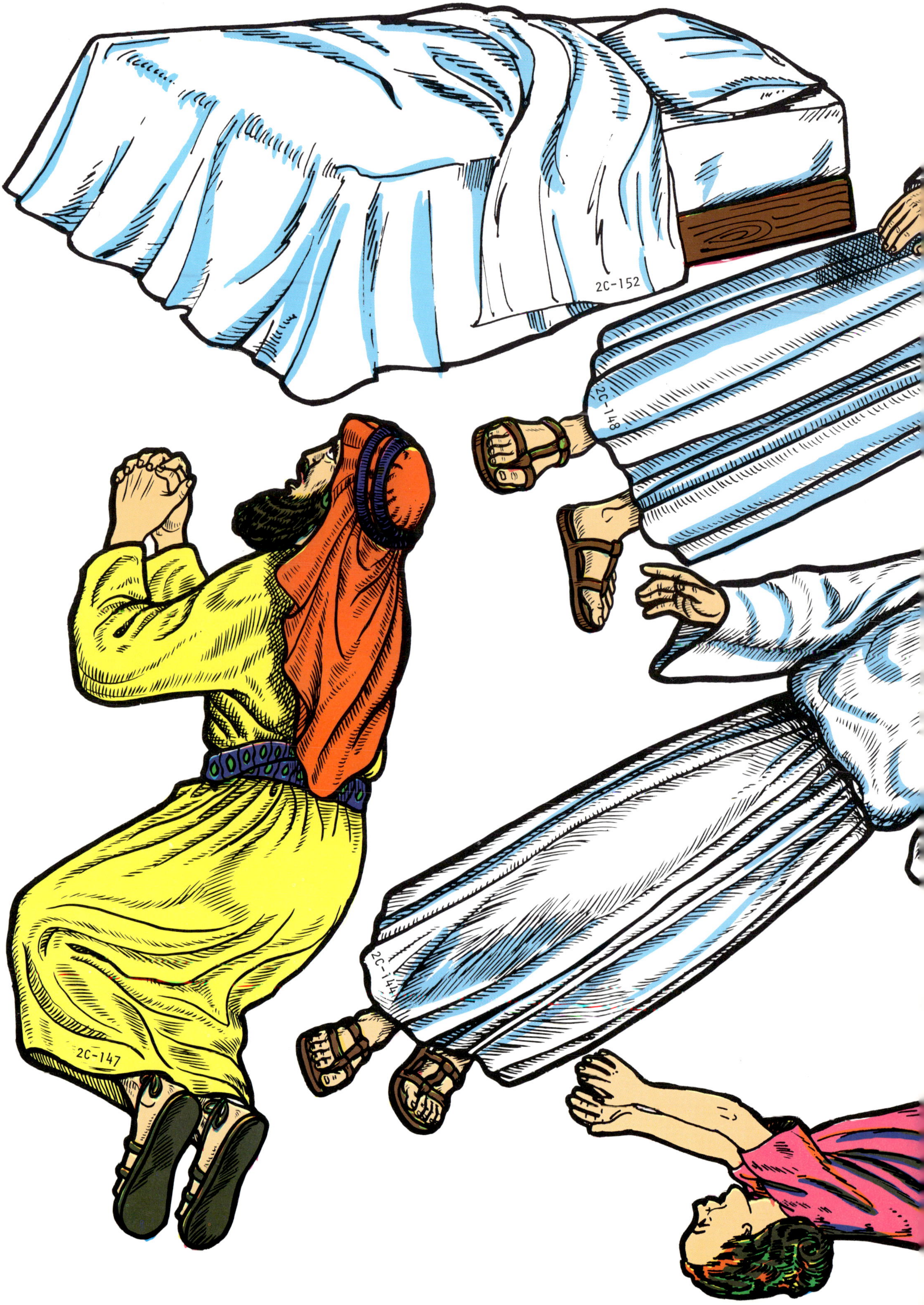
2C-152
2C-148
2C-147
2C-144

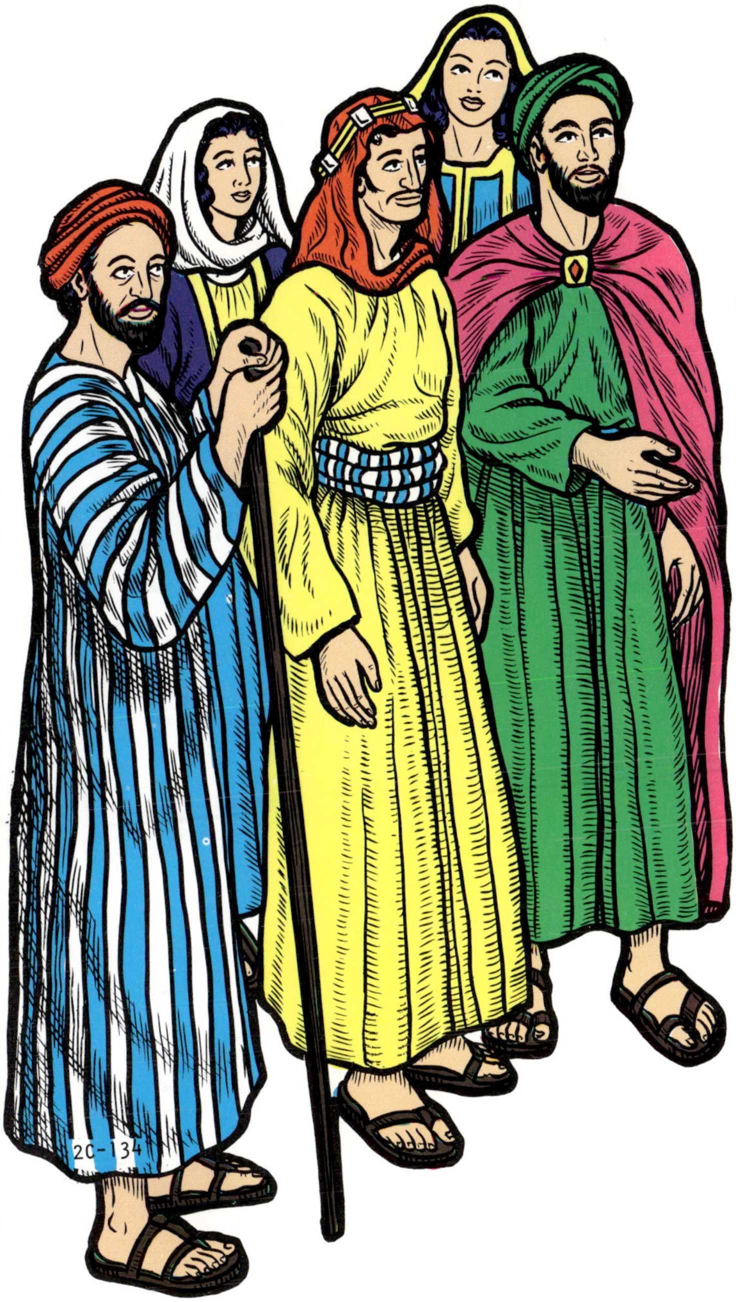
2C-134

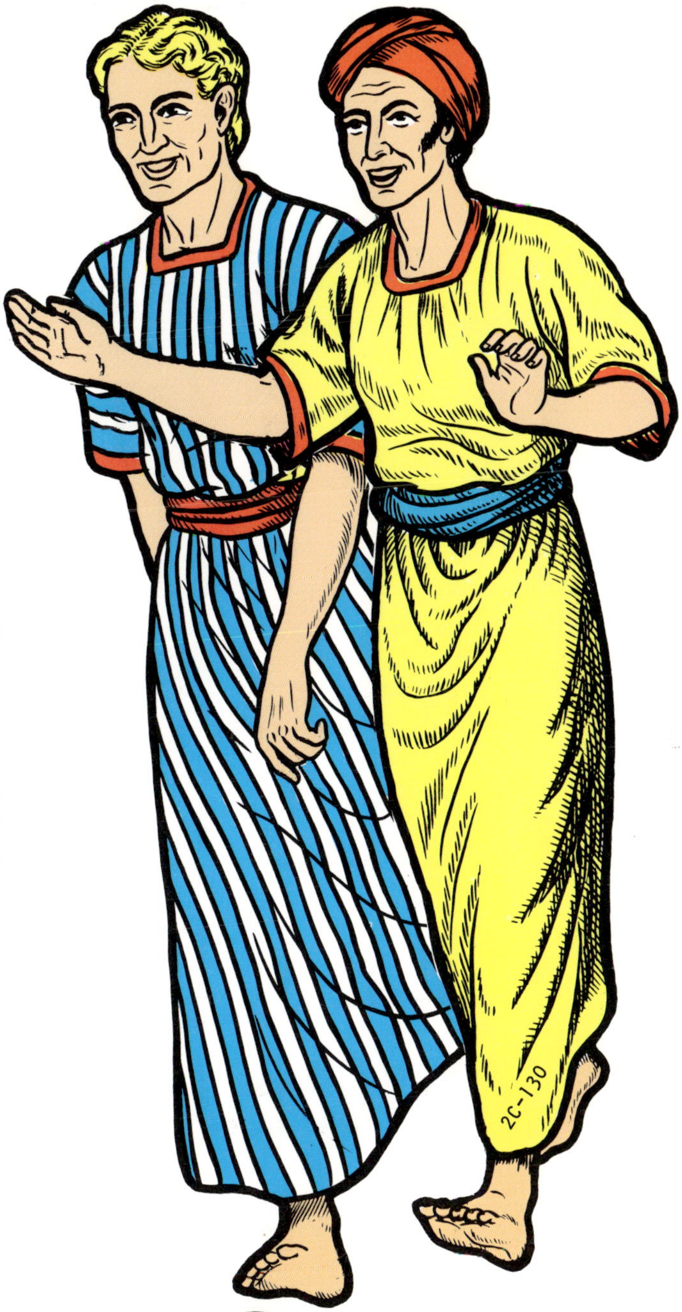
2C-130

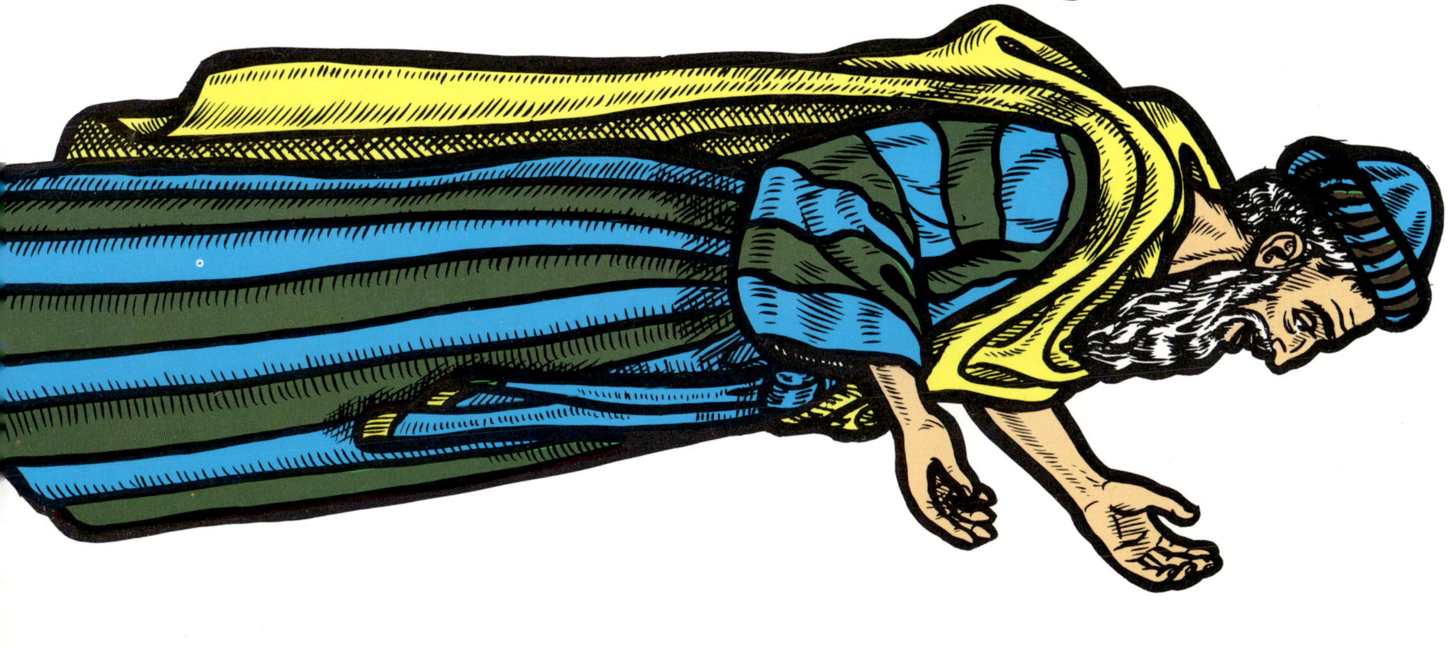

CEF CEF CEF CEF CEF CEF
EF CEF CEF CEF CEF CEF CEF C
F CEF CEF CEF CEF CEF CEF CE
CEF CEF CEF CEF CEF CE
EF CEF CEF CEF CEF CEF C
F CEF CEF CEF CEF CEF CE
CEF CEF CEF CEF CEF CE
EF CEF CEF CEF CEF CEF C
F CEF CEF CEF CEF CEF CE
CEF CEF CEF CEF CEF CE
EF CEF CEF CEF CEF CEF C
F CEF CEF CEF CEF CEF CE
CEF CEF CEF CEF CEF CE
EF CEF CEF CEF CEF CEF C
F CEF CEF CEF CEF CEF CEF

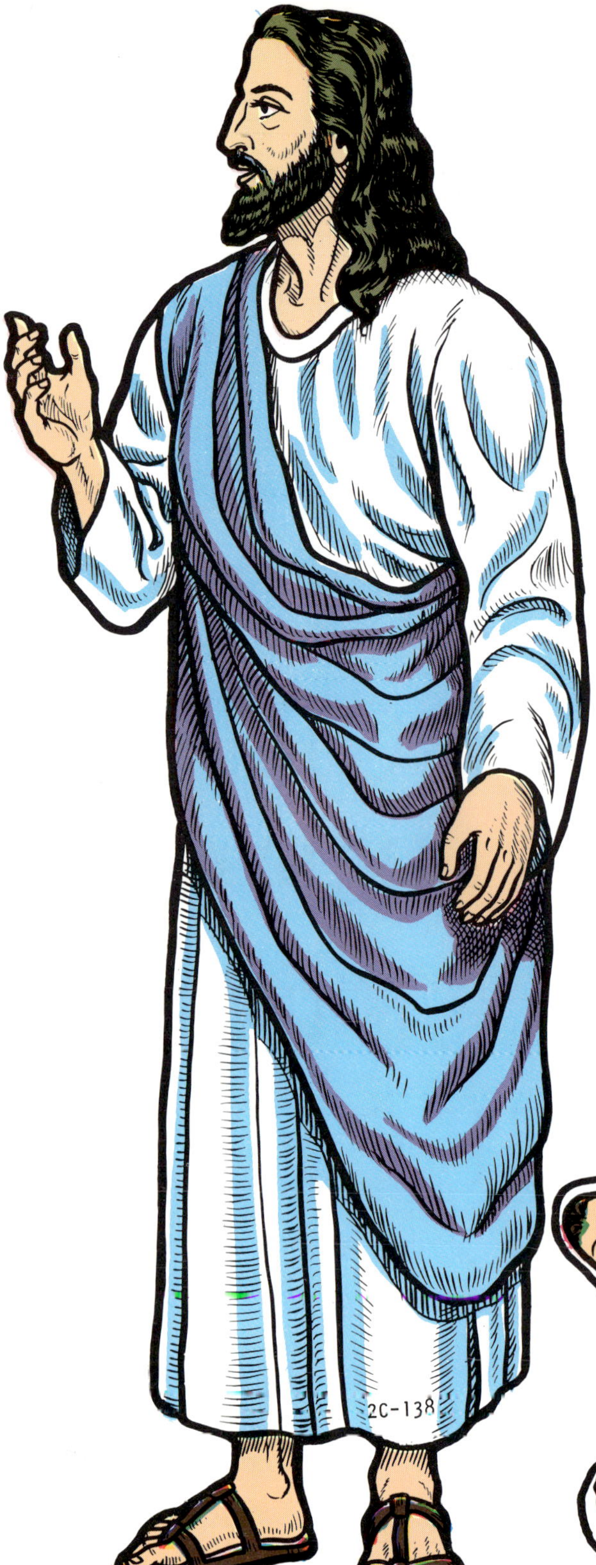
2C-138

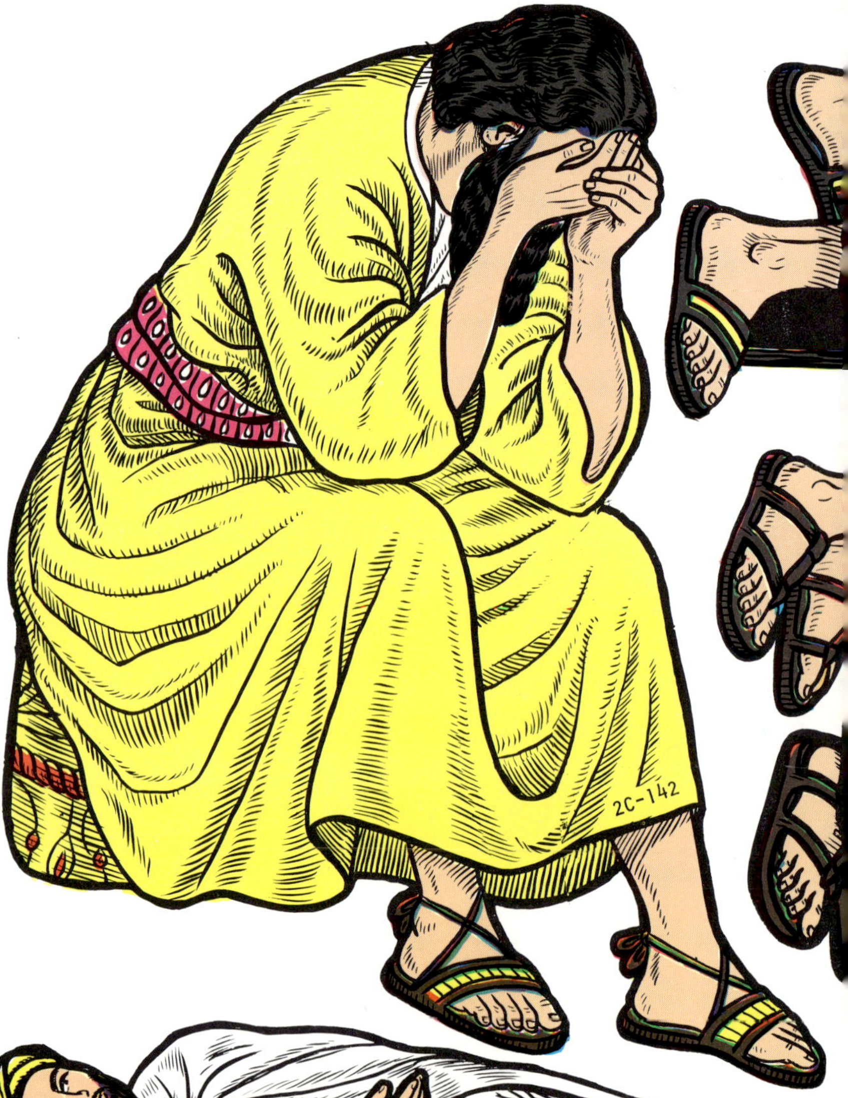
2C-142

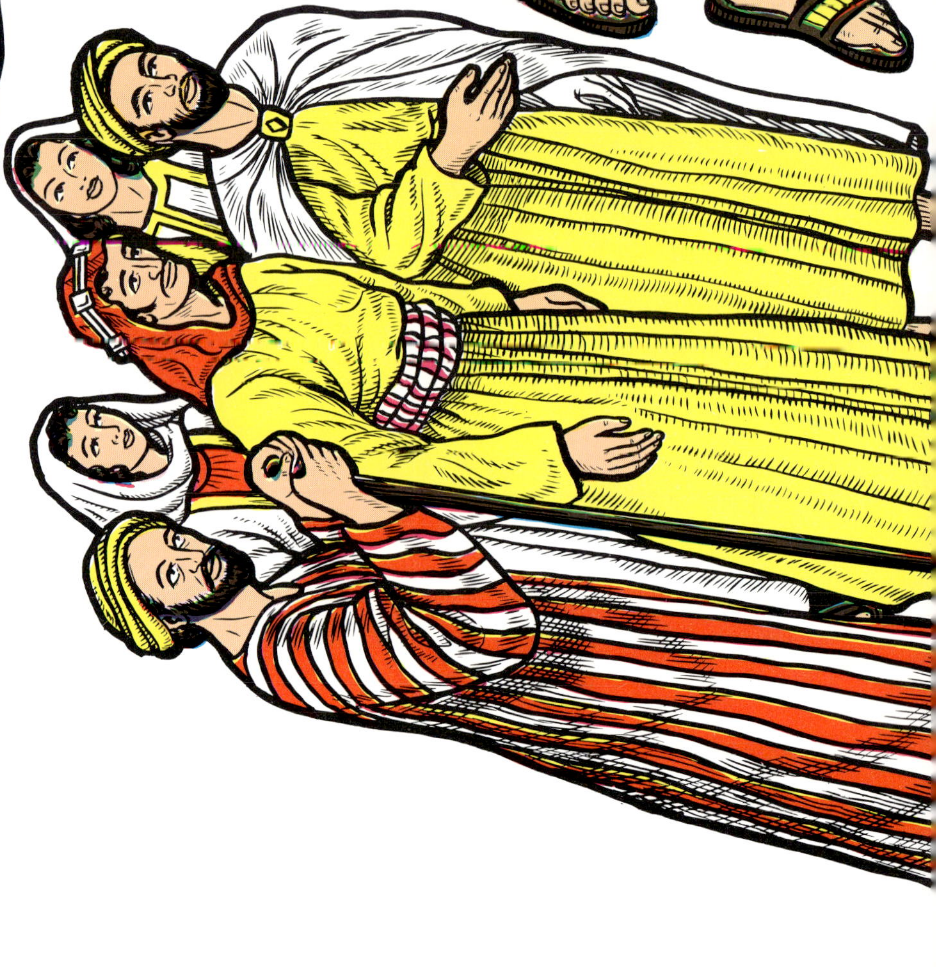

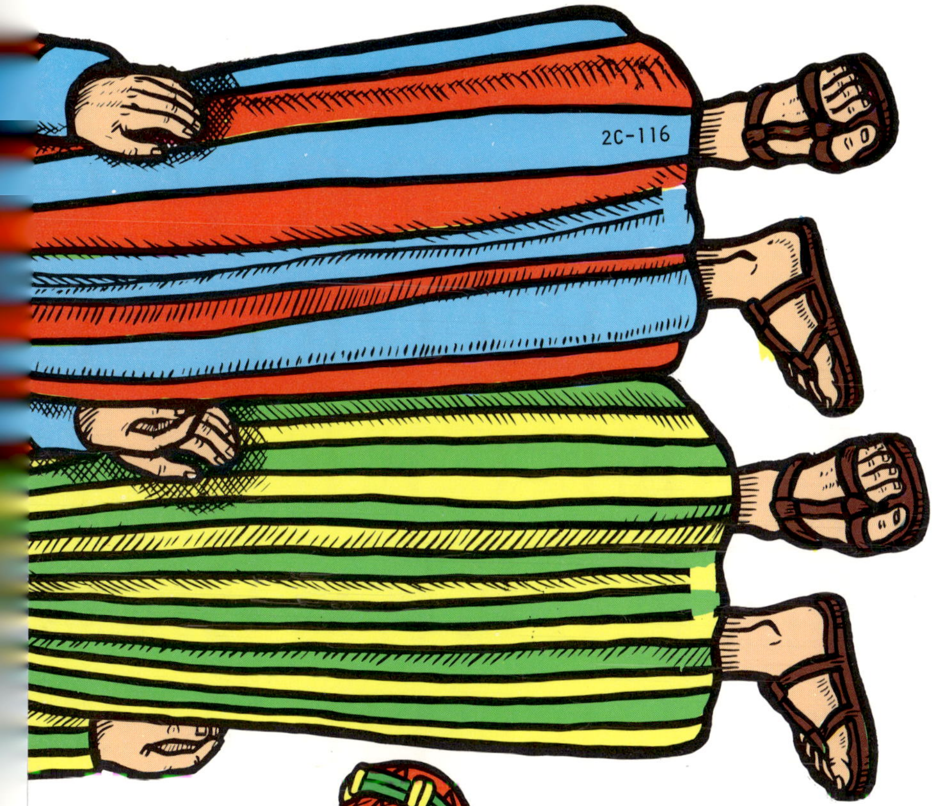
2C-116

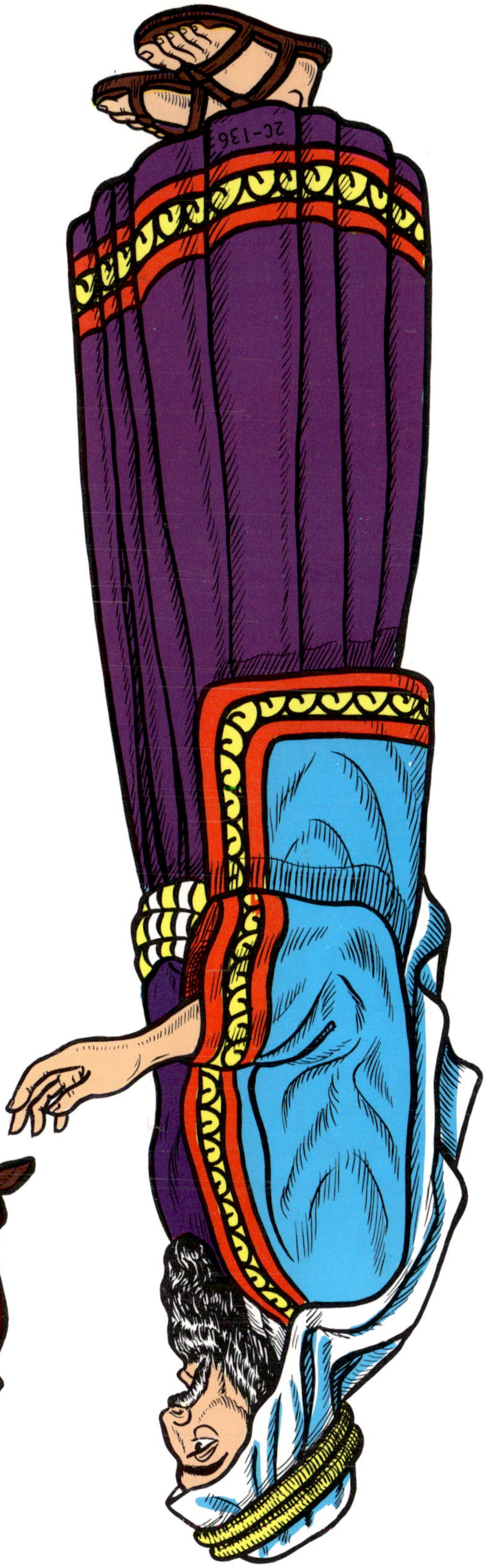
2C-136

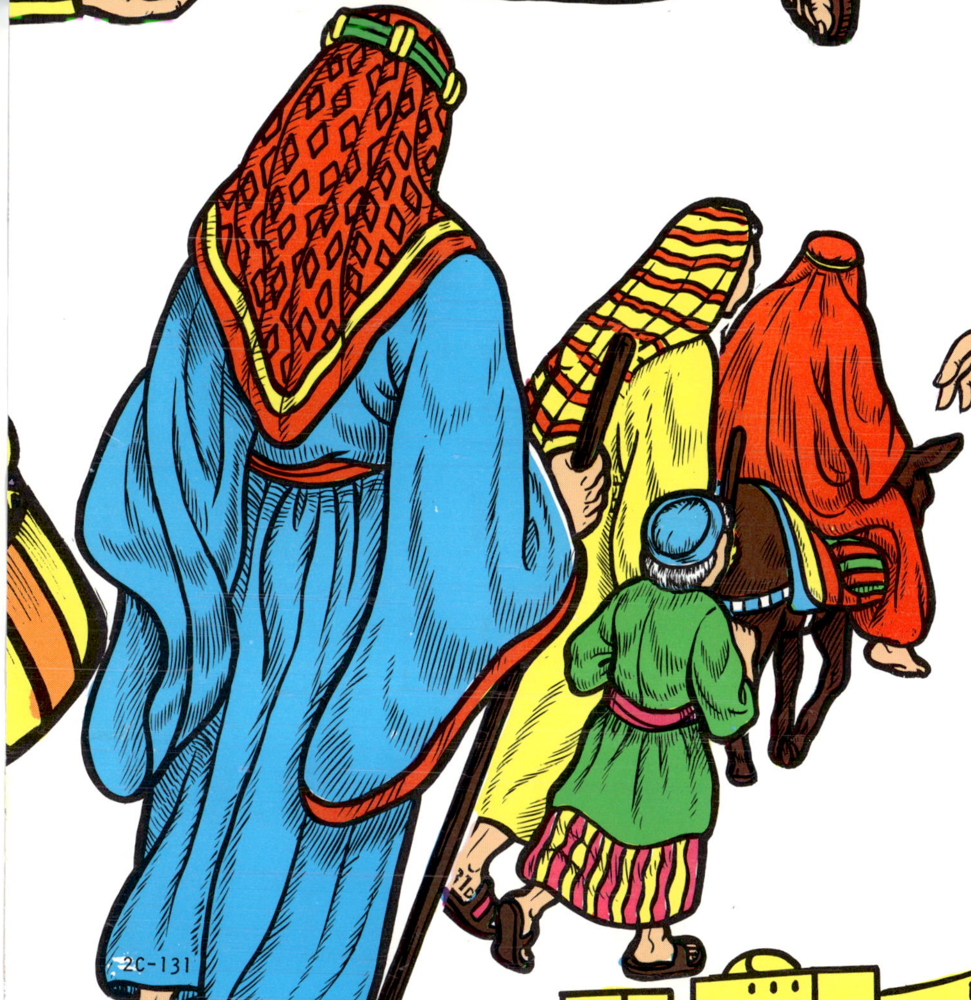
2C-131

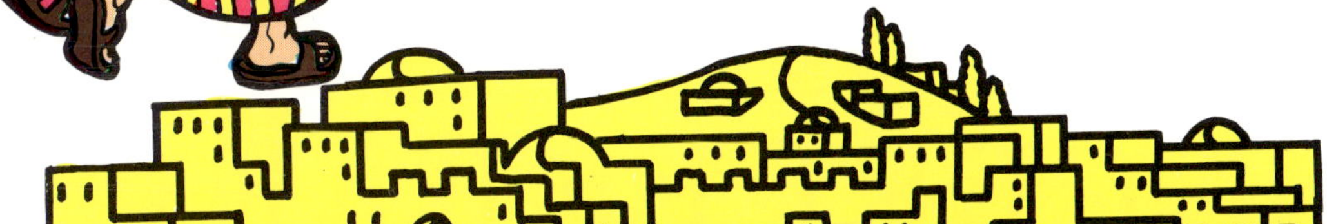
2C-128

2C-113

2C-122

2C-123

CEF CEF CEF CEF CEF CEF CE
EF CEF CEF CEF CEF CEF C
F CEF CEF CEF CEF CEF CE
CEF CEF CEF CEF CEF CE
EF CEF CEF CEF CEF CEF C
F CEF CEF CEF CEF CEF C
CEF CEF CEF CEF CEF CE
EF CEF CEF CEF CEF CEF C
F CEF CEF CEF CEF CEF C
CEF CEF CEF CEF CEF C
EF CEF CEF CEF CEF CEF
F CEF CEF CEF CEF CEF C
CEF CEF CEF CEF CEF C
EF CEF CEF CEF CEF CEF
F CEF CEF CEF CEF CEF C

CEF CEF CEF CEF CEF CEF
EF CEF CEF CEF CEF CEF C
F CEF CEF CEF CEF CEF CE
CEF CEF CEF CEF CEF CEF
EF CEF CEF CEF CEF CEF C
F CEF CEF CEF CEF CEF CE
CEF CEF CEF CEF CEF CEF
EF CEF CEF CEF CEF CEF C
F CEF CEF CEF CEF CEF CE
CEF CEF CEF CEF CEF CEF
F CEF CEF CEF CEF CEF CE
CEF CEF CEF CEF CEF CEF
EF CEF CEF CEF CEF CEF C
F CEF CEF CEF CEF CEF CE

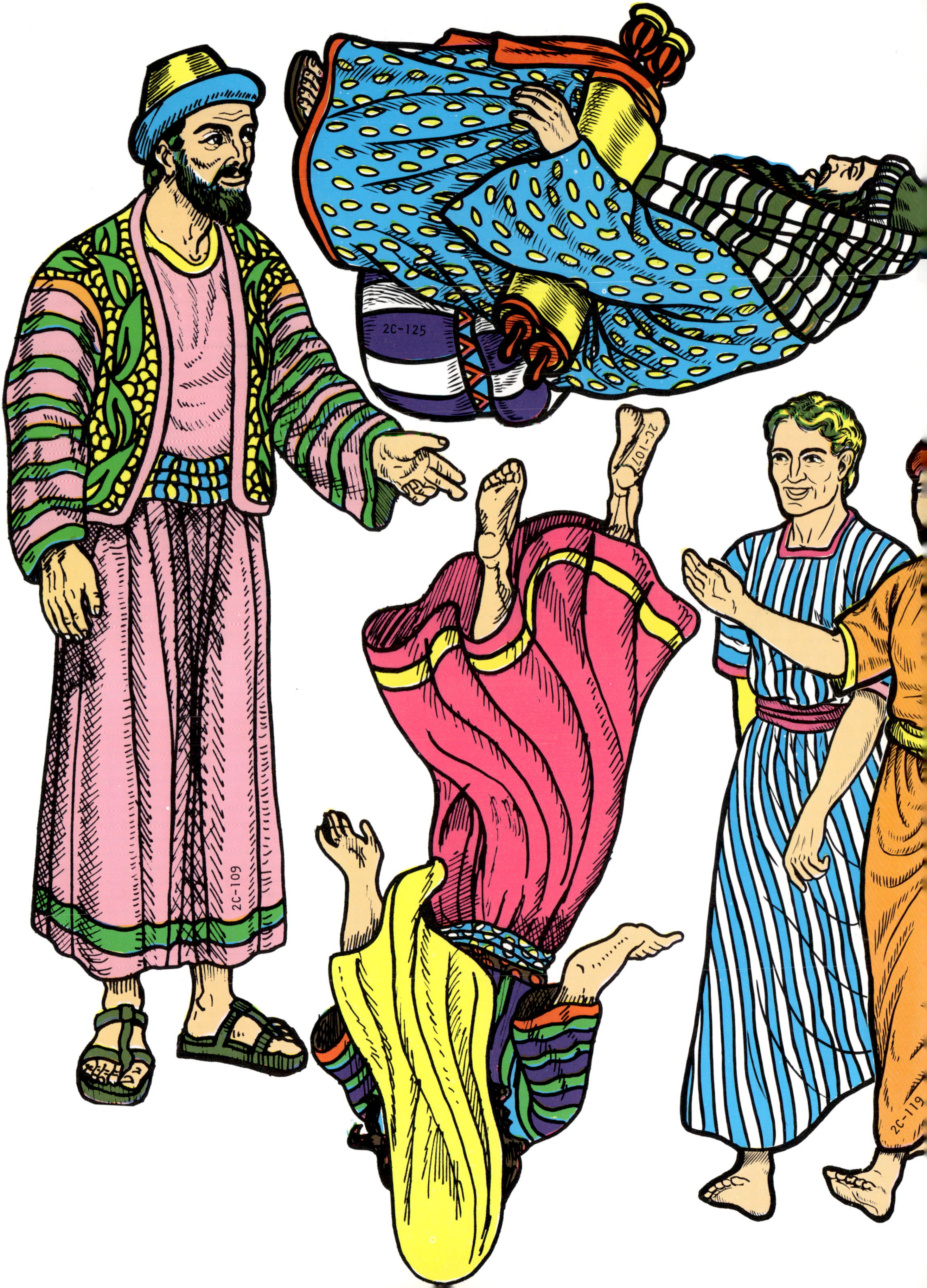
2C-109
2C-125
2C-107
2C-119

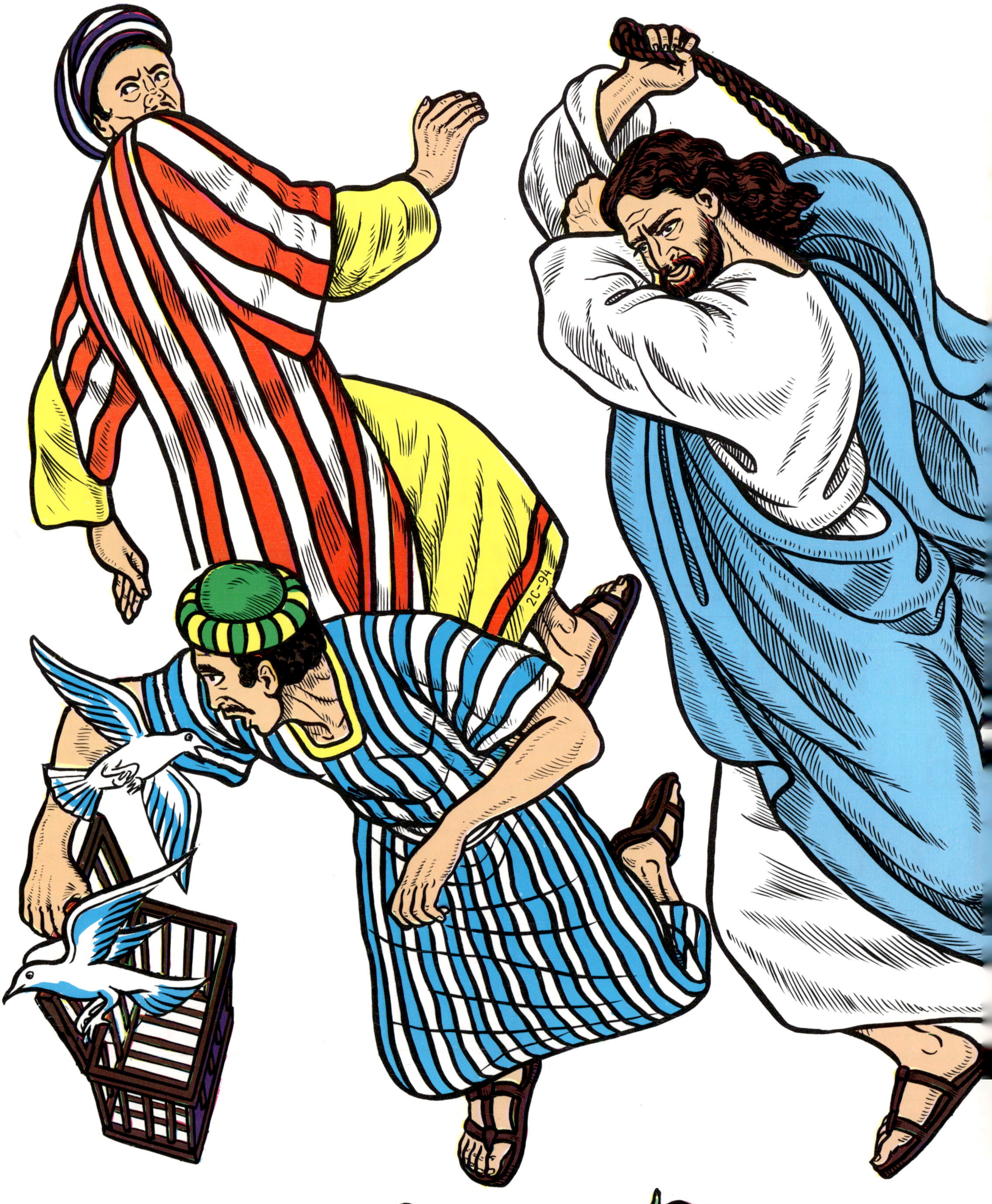
2C-94
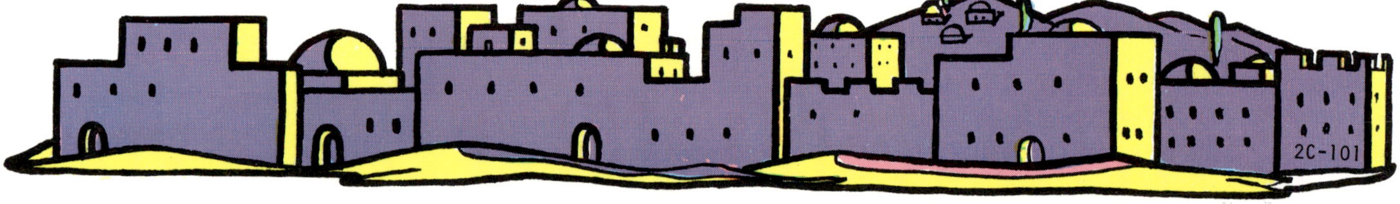
2C-101

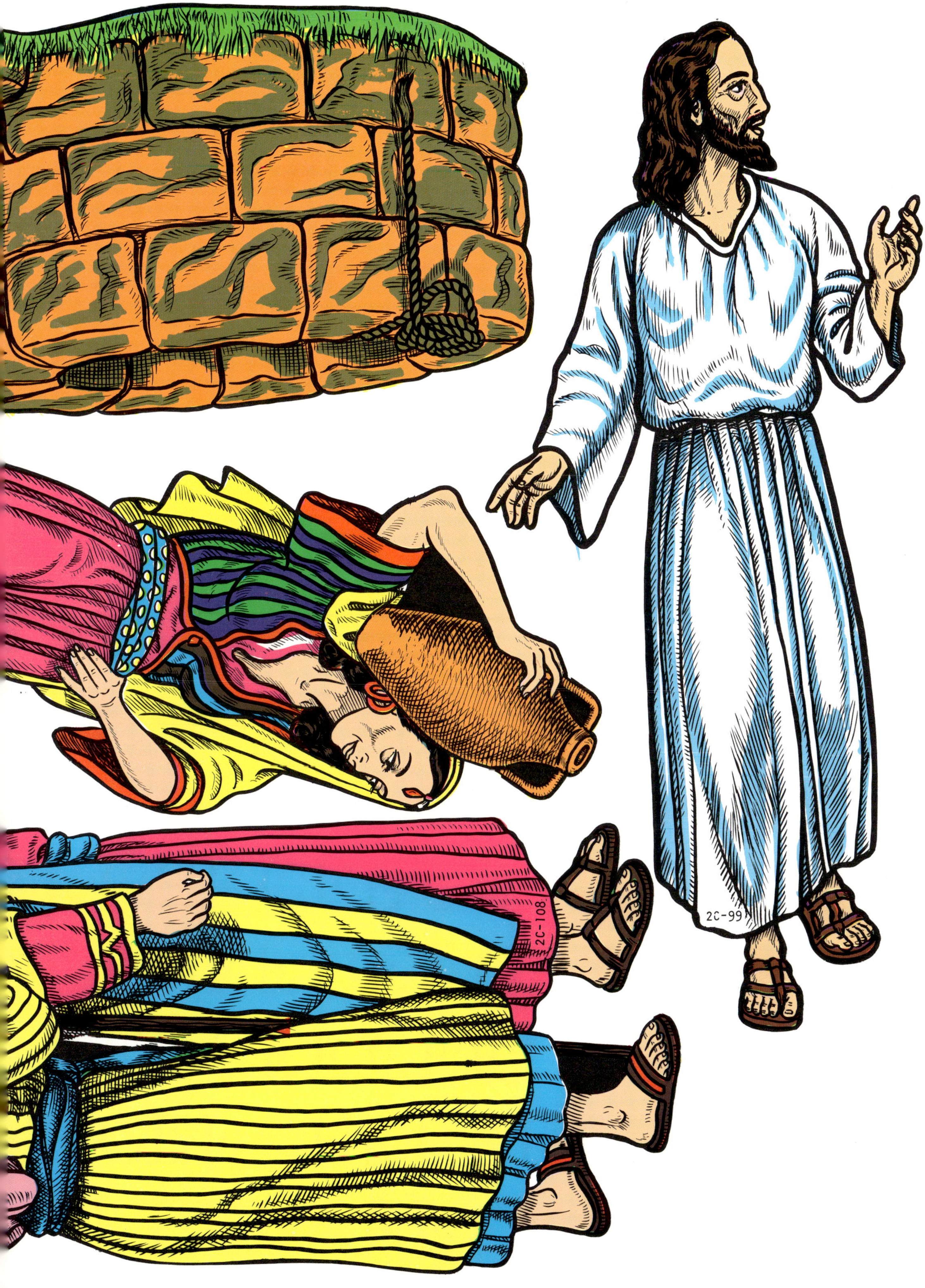
2C-99
2C-108

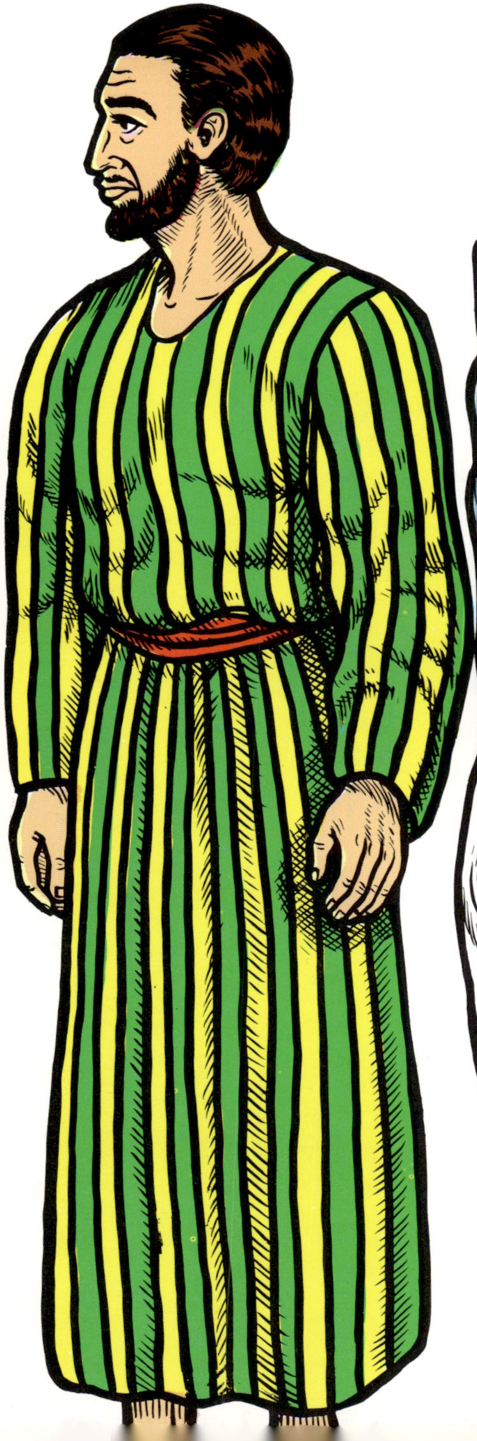

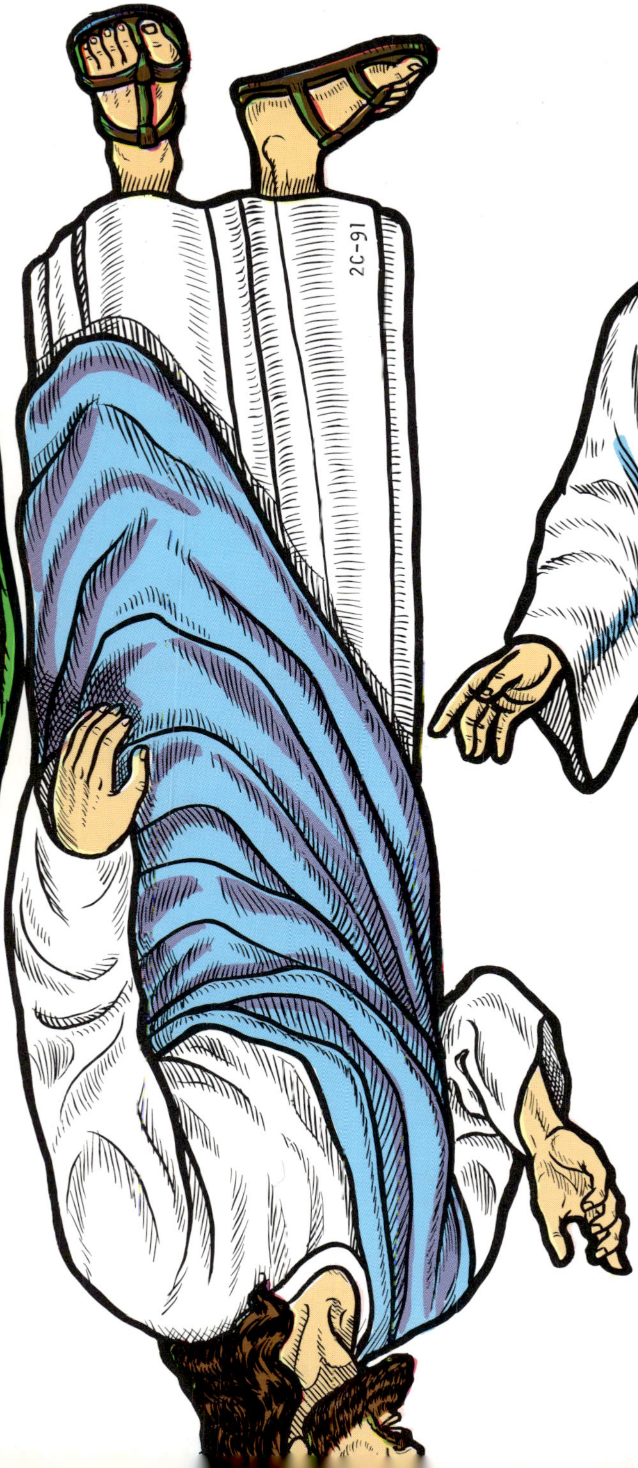
2C-91

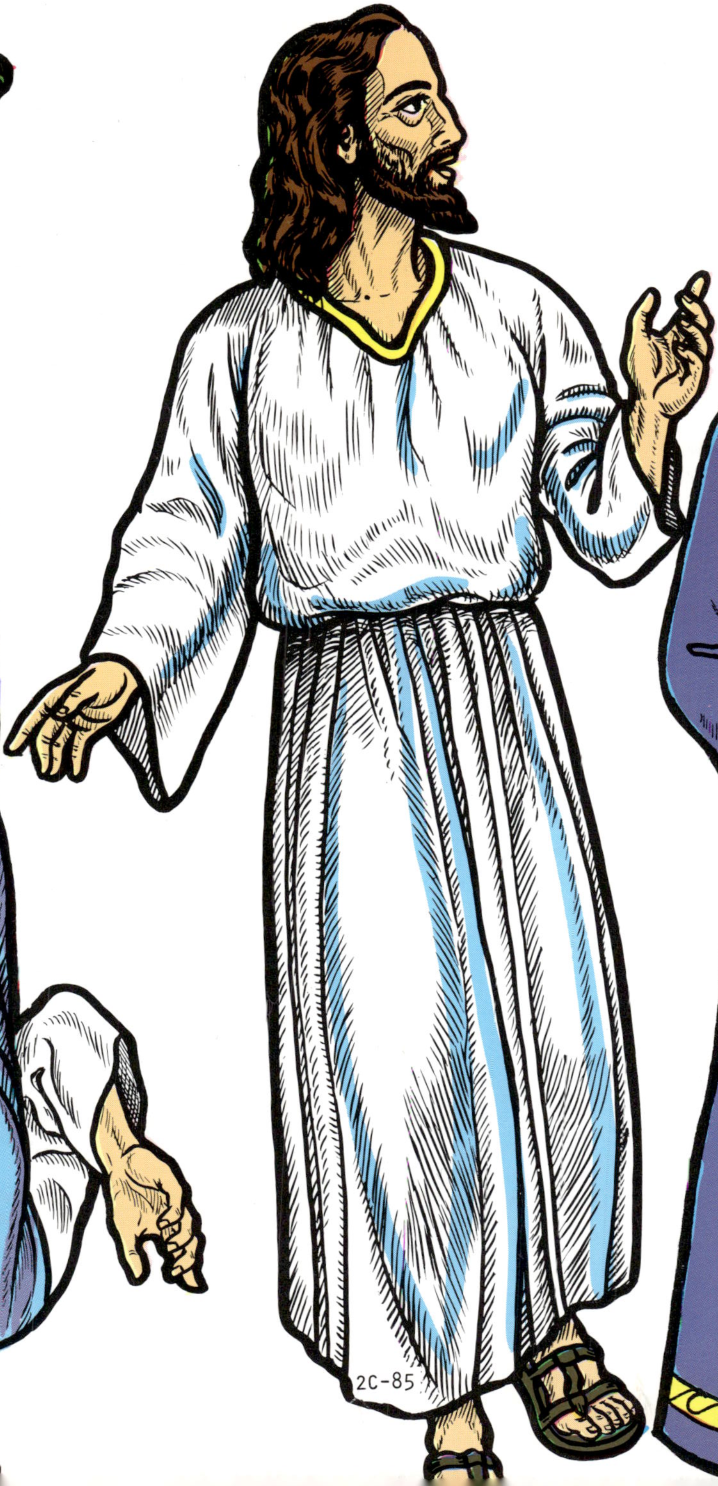
2C-85

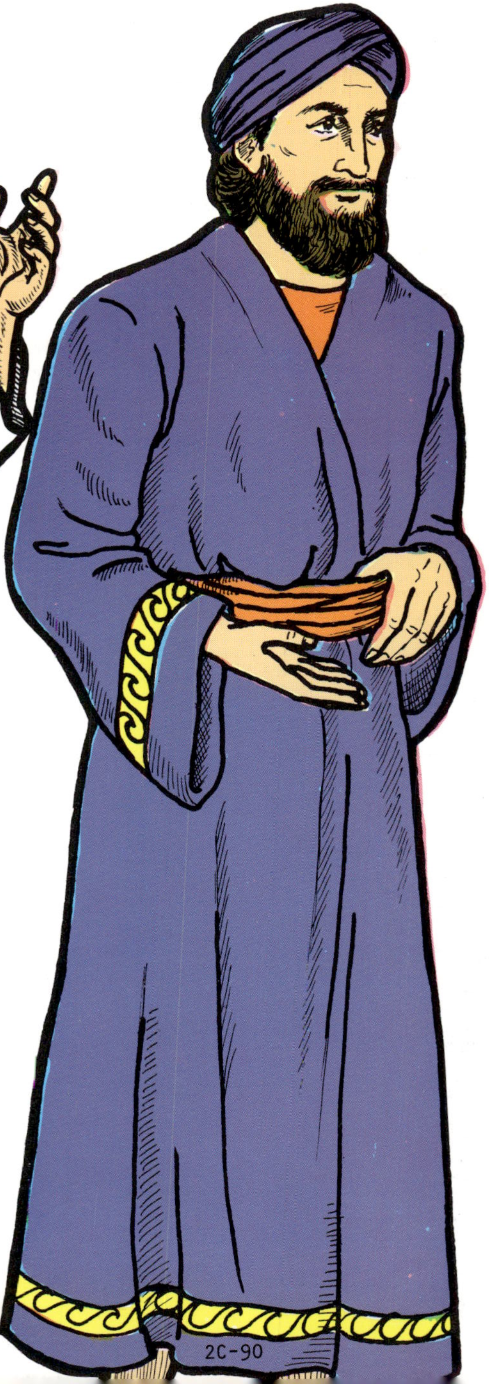
2C-90

CEF CEF CEF CEF CEF CEF
EF CEF CEF CEF CEF CEF C
F CEF CEF CEF CEF CEF CE
CEF CEF CEF CEF CEF CEF
EF CEF CEF CEF CEF CEF C
F CEF CEF CEF CEF CEF CE
CEF CEF CEF CEF CEF CEF
EF CEF CEF CEF CEF CEF C
F CEF CEF CEF CEF CEF CE
CEF CEF CEF CEF CEF CEF
EF CEF CEF CEF CEF CEF C
F CEF CEF CEF CEF CEF CE
CEF CEF CEF CEF CEF CEF
EF CEF CEF CEF CEF CEF C
F CEF CEF CEF CEF CEF CE

CEF CEF CEF CEF CEF CEF
CEF CEF CEF CEF CEF CEF C
CEF CEF CEF CEF CEF CEF CE
CEF CEF CEF CEF CEF CEF
CEF CEF CEF CEF CEF CEF C
CEF CEF CEF CEF CEF CEF CE
CEF CEF CEF CEF CEF CEF
CEF CEF CEF CEF CEF CEF C
CEF CEF CEF CEF CEF CEF CE
CEF CEF CEF CEF CEF CEF
CEF CEF CEF CEF CEF CEF C
CEF CEF CEF CEF CEF CEF CE
CEF CEF CEF CEF CEF CEF
CEF CEF CEF CEF CEF CEF C
CEF CEF CEF CEF CEF CEF CE

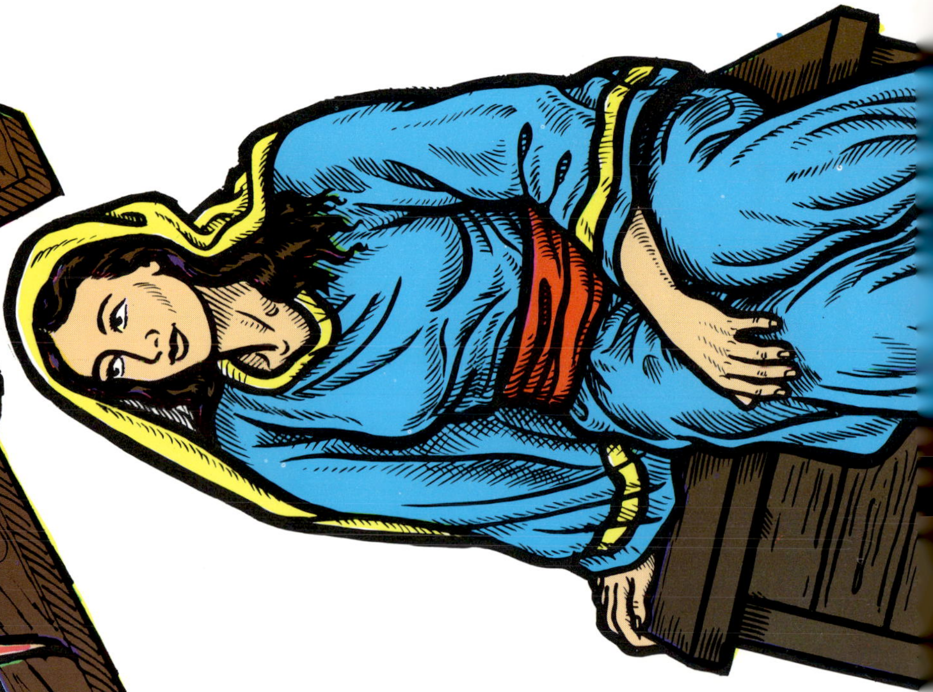

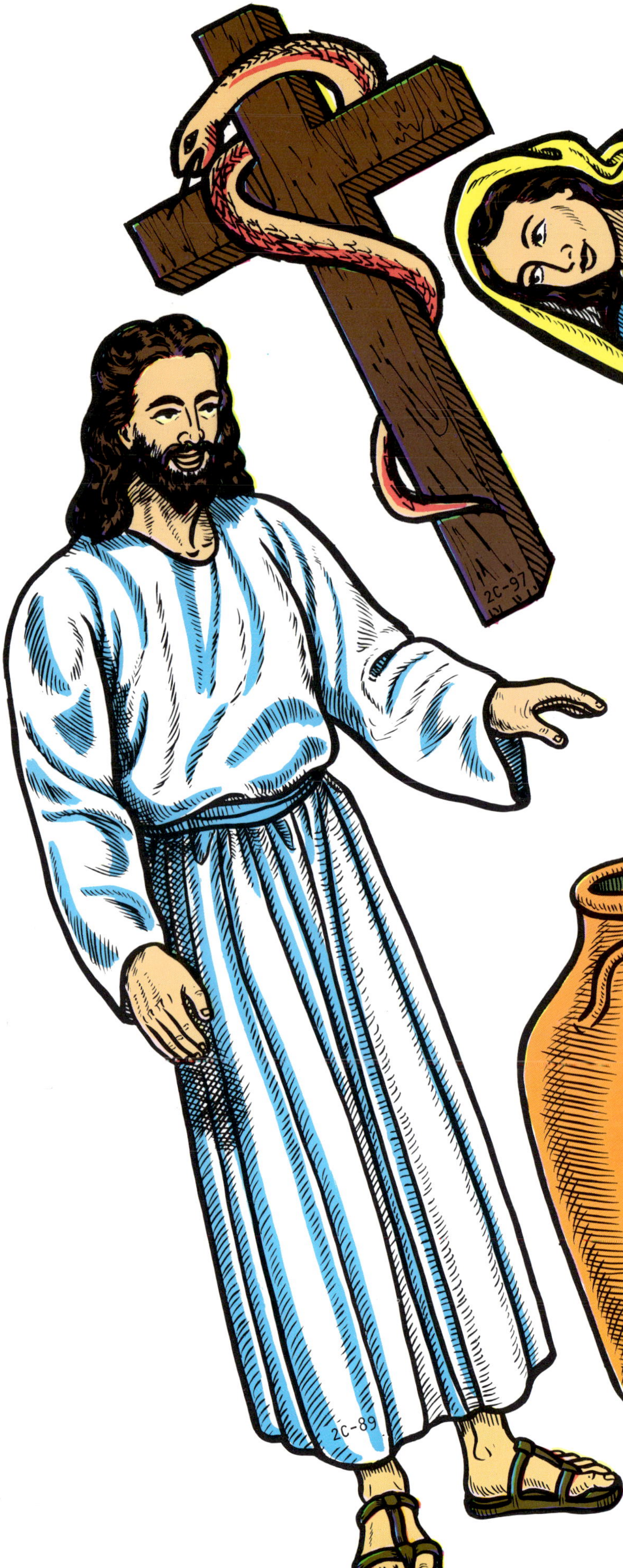
2C-97
2C-89

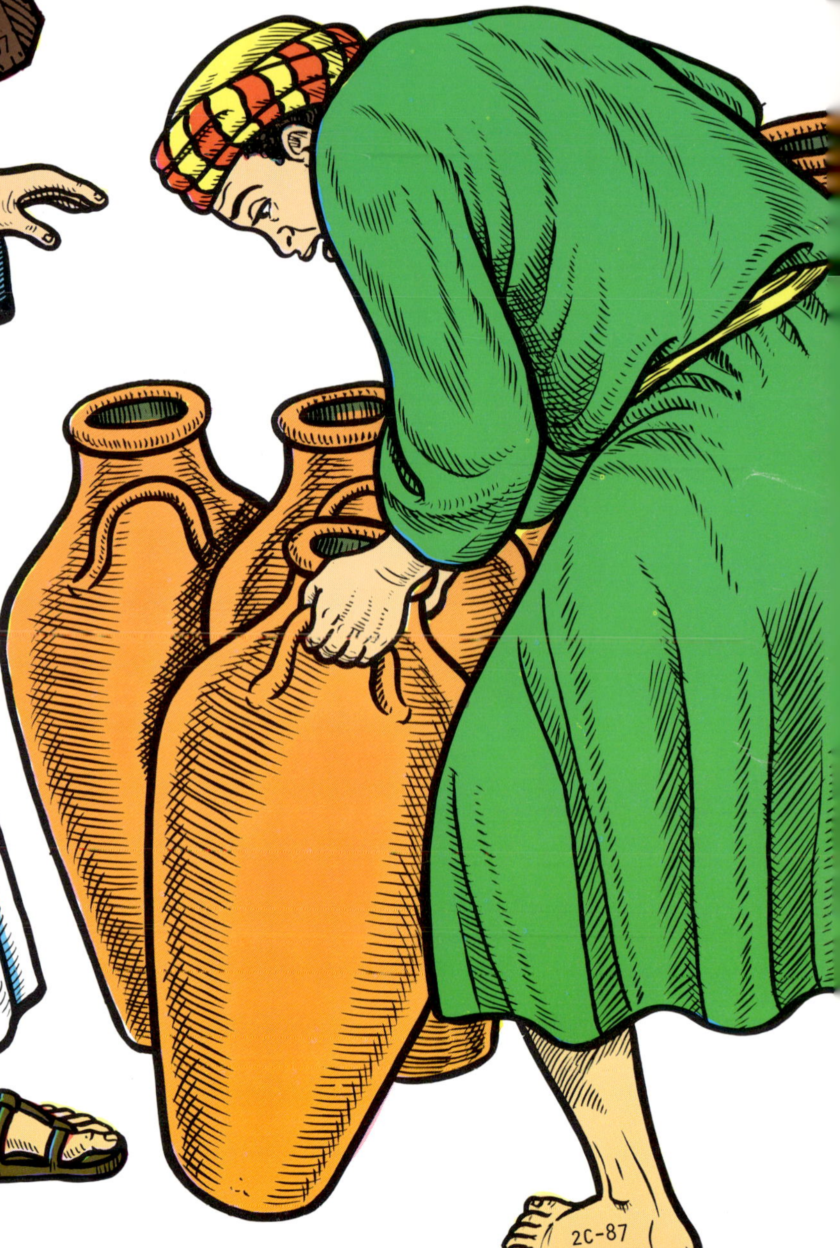
2C-87

Cana. The miles had never seemed so long. Every minute counted. That little boy was dying!
Finally, he arrived. Then, the question, "Where is Jesus?" At last he found Him, perhaps at Nathaniel's house.

Scene 3 (indoor)
(Place Christ and disciples, figures 2C-111 and 2C-116. Add nobleman, 2C-117)

The boy's father began to beg and plead with the Lord Jesus. "Please come to my house immediately and heal my son, for he is dying."
But, the Lord Jesus did not hurry away with him. "You people will not believe unless you see lots of miracles," Jesus said.
Did the Lord Jesus not care about the little boy? Did He not feel sorry for the man who was so worried? Yes, He did care. He loved him very much. Just as He loves you very much, and cares about you. He just wanted that man to truly love and trust Him . . . to believe and receive Him as the Son of God.
The man could think only about his son. "Sir", he begged, "Please come with me right away before my child dies."
"You may go home and don't worry anymore. Your son will live!" the Lord Jesus said.
Do you think the man kept pleading with Him? Did He say, "How can my son get well if You don't come and see him?" No! He just believed and received the word of the Lord.
Sometimes you and I do not take God at His Word. He does not answer a prayer right away. He does not do something exactly the way you expect Him to do it. So, you doubt Him; and sometimes I do, too. He wants us to receive His Word and trust Him.
(Remove figures)

Scene 4 (outdoor)
(Place nobleman, 2C-118)

The rich man started home to Capernaum right away, because he trusted the word of the Lord Jesus. It was such a long trip. He could not get home the same day. Night came and he had to wait until morning. When it began to get light he was on his way again.
(Place servants 2C-119)

He was still some distance from Capernaum when he saw some servants from his house coming to meet him.
They hurried to exclaim, "Your son is alive and well!"
"When did he begin to feel better?" the father asked.
"Yesterday at one o'clock the fever left him," they answered.
The man knew it was exactly that time when the Lord Jesus said, "Your son will live!"

Scene 5 (outdoor)
(Add nobleman's son and wife, 2C-120 and 2C-121)

What a happy time it was when the father reached home. The most wonderful thing of all is that the Bible says, "The man and his whole household believed in the Lord Jesus." They were ready to *receive* Him. (Show wordstrip) The nobleman's wife, his son, his servants, all of them, with the man himself, believed in the Lord Jesus as the very Son of God. They knew Jesus loved them and cared for them, and they could go to Him with any need. You can trust Him with your needs, too.

(Remove figures)

The Bible says this was the second miracle Jesus did after He came back into Galilee. Some people were beginning to be very curious about Him. *Who was this "miracle worker,"* they wondered. Then the Lord Jesus went to Nazareth, the town where He lived as a boy . . . the place of Joseph's carpenter shop.

Scene 6 (temple scene)
On the day of worship, called the Sabbath day, Jesus went to the place of worship, called the synagogue.
(Place scribes 2C-124, 125; pulpit, 2C-123)

Since the leaders in the synagogue knew He was a teacher they asked Him to take part in the service. They handed Him a scroll to read. (Teacher, explain "scroll" if necessary.) It was the part of our Bible called the book of Isaiah.
(Place figure of Christ in pulpit, 2C-122, removing 2C-123)

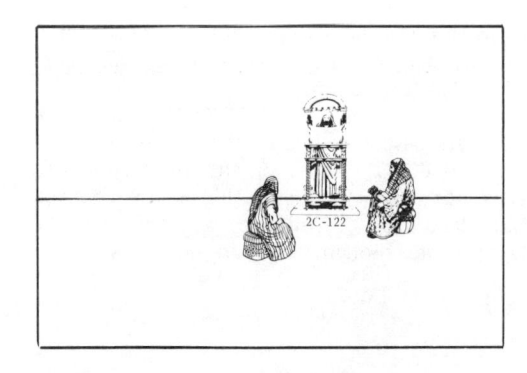

The Lord Jesus opened the scroll to what we call chapter 61 of Isaiah and began to read at verse 1. This is what the Lord Jesus read. (Teacher: Read from Isaiah 61:1,2a.)

17

Scene 7 (temple scene)
(Replace figure 2C-122 with 2C-123; place figure of Christ, 2C-126)

He handed the scroll to the man who was waiting to take it and sat down. (It was the custom to stand up to read and sit down to speak.) The crowd in the synagogue listened to hear what He would say. "This very day this Scripture which I read is coming true; right here and right now," He said. He meant that He was the person of whom Isaiah wrote, almost 700 years before that day. As He read that Scripture He was reading about Himself. As He went on speaking the people understood that, and were amazed at the beautiful words He spoke.
"Is this not Joseph's son?" they asked.
How would you have answered that? "Not Joseph's son, but God's Son. Not just a great man, but the Son of God from Heaven."
The Lord Jesus said to them, "You would probably like to say to me, 'Prove it if you are someone special. Do the miracles here in your home town that you did in Capernaum.' Then He added, "No prophet is welcomed in his home town." He knew they would think of Him only as Joseph's son and not receive Him as the Son of God sent to be their Saviour from sin. He knew they would refuse Him. Do you know that the very worst sin is to refuse the Lord Jesus Christ?
(Show wordstrip refuse)
We think of sins like murder and kidnapping and violent crimes. But even though you could not think of one wrong thing you had done, God still says you are a sinner! God's Word says we were born in sin (Psalm 51:5). When Jesus Christ died on the cross He paid the price for all sins. Every sin can be forgiven through His blood. Your sins of meanness, disobedience, lying, fighting, (and the ones you are thinking about that I haven't named), can be forgiven because the Lord Jesus died and rose again that you might have forgiveness of sin.
When you *receive* Him you have forgiveness, no matter what sins you have done. As long as you continue to *refuse* Him you can never have His forgiveness.
The Lord Jesus then reminded those people that their relatives who lived years before had refused to listen to God's prophets, Elijah and Elisha. "So God sent the prophets to people who were not Jews and these other people received them," He said, "and God did miracles for those who received His prophets even though they were not Jews, or the people of Israel."
(Remove figures)

Scene 8 (outdoor)
(Place figure 2C-127)

When the listeners in the synagogue heard those words they were furious. To think that He would suggest that God would do great things for people who were not Jews! They were very proud of their nationality and would never admit that God loved others as much as He did them. They were so angry that all together they jumped up and pushed Jesus Christ out of the synagogue into the street. They kept pushing Him all the way out of town . . . to the edge of a cliff. The Bible says they planned to throw Him over the cliff. But suddenly . . . miraculously . . . He escaped!
(Remove figure)
They couldn't hold Him and He was gone. They did not expect that kind of miracle!
"He came unto his own . . . ." In our lesson it was His own town; His own people. ". . . and his own received him not." They refused Him. Are you not glad for the next word? *"But"* . . . yes, there is something else. "But as many as received him to them gave he power to become the sons of God . . . ."
Will you *refuse* or *receive*? (Teacher: point to wordstrips).
If you *refuse* Him then He must *refuse* you. You cannot be where He is, in Heaven. If you *receive* Him, He will *receive* you to be with Him forever.
You may have already received Him, but if not, will you do that right now? "Lord Jesus, I don't want to say 'no' to You any longer. I want to say 'yes.' I do receive You as my Saviour from sin because I believe You died for me." If this is your desire today, I want to talk with you after class so you may understand better what it means to receive the Lord Jesus.
For you who have received Him, He wants to help in whatever need you have. You can tell Him about your need. Maybe your need is to love someone who is not a very nice person. Or, you may need to understand and enjoy a certain subject in school. Or, you might need help to obey. Or, some need that I couldn't possibly think of . . . that only you know. You have received Him. He will not refuse you help when you need Him.
As we pray, think of some need that you have and pray about that. All of us do have needs. I have some, too. (Have a few moments of silent prayer.) There is a place on your memory token to write out a special need you have, to help you remember to pray about that need this week. When we return to class next time I'm sure you will have something to share about the way God met your need. I am sure that I can share with you then about some need He has met for me.
(Remind children of area for counseling)

LESSON ELEVEN

MIRACLE OUTSIDE JERICHO
(Blind Bartimaeus Made To See)

Scripture
Mark 10:46-52; Luke 18:35-43

Aim
That the child may learn to know and follow the Lord Jesus as the light of his life.

Memory Verse
John 8:12 — "I am the light of the world. He that followeth me shall not walk in darkness but shall have the light of life."

Teaching the Memory Verse
What does light do? (If possible, use some visual illustration of light illuminating the darkness.) Light shows up things that can be hidden by darkness. The Lord Jesus said He was the light of the world. Does that mean the world is in darkness? Yes, the whole world of people has been in what the Bible calls "darkness of sin." The Bible says in Romans 3:23, ". . . all have sinned." In what way is the Lord Jesus a light to the *world?* He was the only person who ever lived in this world in whose life there was no sin. So, His perfect life shows up sin in our lives as light shows up things hidden by darkness. Beside the perfect life of the Lord Jesus, your sin looks very dark.

In this verse the Lord Jesus says, "he that followeth me shall not walk in darkness." What does it mean to follow Him? You can receive the Lord Jesus as your Saviour and trust Him to show you the right way to live, the way to please Him. His words and His life are your guide. They show you what to do as you follow Him. If you have trusted Him as your Saviour from sin, He is your light of life.

Visual Aids
Flannel background: outdoor with figures 2C-128—2C-139. Visuals for songs "Trust and Obey" and "The Light of the World is Jesus," are available from Bible Visuals, Inc., P. O. Box Z, Akron, Pennsylvania 17501. Use John 1:12 memory aid from last week's lesson for song visual.

Suggested Songs
Salvation Songs Number 1: "Thy Word Have I Hid in Mine Heart," No. 71; "The Light of the World Is Jesus," No. 99
Salvation Songs Number 2: "John 1:12," No. 79
Salvation Songs Number 3: "Trust and Obey," No. 49
Salvation Songs Number 4: "I Have Decided to Follow Jesus," No. 76

Schedule For Teaching
Song — "I Have Decided to Follow Jesus"
Song — "Thy Word Have I Hid in Mine Heart"
Verse Review
Song — "John 1:12"
Lesson Review
Song — "Trust and Obey"
Teach Memory Verse — John 8:12
Song — "The Light of the World Is Jesus"
Bible Lesson — "Miracle Outside Jericho"
Application of the Truth

Review
Instigate a special *verse* review. For variation make a target for flannelboard, using three colors of flannel. (Approximate size: large circle, 9 inches in diameter; medium circle, 6 inches in diameter; small circle, 3 inches in diameter.) Make small arrows from two colors of construction paper. Divide group into teams, assigning one color of arrows to each team. Give references to teams alternately. If verse is quoted correctly place arrow in center circle and score 10 points for team. If verse is nearly correct place on next circle and score five points. If verse is totally incorrect, but pupil has tried,

place arrow on outer circle and score one point. Leave all arrows on target until end of quiz, counting total score of each side as you remove them.

Review Questions
1. Give me two words showing a contrast in John 1:11, 12.
A. Refuse and Receive.
2. What big need did the man from Capernaum have?
A. His little son was very sick.
3. Why did he go to Jesus with his need?
A. He had heard about the miracles of the Lord Jesus and believed He could help.
4. What did Jesus tell him?
A. "Go home. Your son will live."
5. What happened in that family because of this?
A. Everyone in that house received the Lord Jesus.
6. After this the Lord Jesus went to His home town. What town was that?
A. Nazareth.
7. How did the people in the synagogue at Nazareth act toward Him?
A. They refused Him and tried to push Him over a cliff.
8. Why did they do this?
A. They did not believe He was the Son of God. They did not think they needed Him.
9. What is the very worst sin?
A. Refusing the Lord Jesus.
10. Discussion question: What special need did you write out and pray about last week? What did God do for you?

Lesson
Close your eyes, everyone, until I count to ten. (Teacher, count slowly.)
What could you see with your eyes closed?
Nothing? Do you think you could have found your way to me with your eyes closed?
You probably could have done that, because you knew where I was standing. (Choose one student.) Jimmy, may I put this blindfold on you? (Blindfold student and take him back to his chair.)
Now, I am going to walk away from you. I will not talk. I will move quietly, and I want you to find me. The other members of the class will tell you when I am ready.
(Permit clubber to try to find you, unless he realizes he probably cannot, as you will keep moving out of his range. After a short time, stop him.)
You cannot find me, Jimmy, because I keep moving away from you. There is just one way you could find me. Do you know what that way is?
(Help children to see that Jimmy could find you only if he had a guide. Remove blindfold.)
We learned from our verse that we have Jesus to guide us. Let's learn in what special way he guided a man in our lesson today.

Scene 1 (outdoor background)
(Place figures 2C-128, city, and 2C-129, Bartimaeus)

A man was seated by the side of the road at the edge of the city of Jericho. Jericho was a pretty city. But, the man could not see the tall palm trees swaying in the breeze. He could not see the rose gardens and other flowers that bloomed throughout the city. He could smell the fragrance of the flowers and the fragrance of the balsam plants growing nearby. But, he could not see them. For the man, Bartimaeus, was blind.
Bartimaeus was not only blind. He was poor. Being blind, he could not work.
Today there are many things a blind person can do. He can learn to read. How does a blind person read? He reads by feeling little bumps on the page. It is called Braille writing. A blind person can learn to type and do many things with his hands. Some blind people have specially trained dogs to be their guides. But, in the time that Bartimaeus lived, there was just about one thing a blind man could do. He could beg. The Bible says Bartimaeus was a beggar.
The life of Bartimaeus was possibly like this: Day after day he sat by the road that went into Jericho. He got people to notice him by calling, "Bakshish! Bakshish!" That means, "Please, a gift. Do you have a tip for me?" Over and over again as Bartimaeus heard footsteps coming he called for help.
(Place figures of travelers, 2C-130, 2C-131, and 2C-134)

Scene 2 (outdoor background)
The entrance to Jericho was a good place for Bartimaeus because Jericho was a very busy city. People were going and coming every hour of the day. Some of them stopped and looked at the ragged beggar.
Bartimaeus probably had a cup in which to collect coins. When someone stopped he waited for the jingle of a coin in his cup. He called "God bless you" as his thanks. Many times, he listened sadly as the steps moved away and there was no "bakshish."
Bartimaeus learned to recognize the footsteps of his friends. Sometimes, even before he heard a voice, he knew there would be a "bakshish" in his cup. Bartimaeus did not forget to call his thanks. But, do you know, he must have been much more thankful for the friend than he was for the money. Are there times that you are a friend to someone in need?
"Bartimaeus," a friend may have called, "did you hear the news?" It was then that Bartimaeus learned of things which were happening in the city and country round about.
Bartimaeus must have had friends who guided him to his home at night and again to his spot by the side of the road in the morning.
(Remove travelers)
It is very hard to always have to depend on someone else. Bartimaeus must have thought, *If only I could help myself. If only I could see. Then, I would not have to trouble someone to guide me.*
Bartimaeus had lots of time to think. He knew about God, so he surely thought about Him. Perhaps he sometimes wondered if God cared that he was blind. Maybe he even

wondered why God would let him be blind if He really loved him.
Did God love him? Of course, He did. God loved Bartimaeus, just as He loves you and me. God loves every person. And, He loves us just the way we are.

(Place figure, 2C-133, friend)

One day an exciting thing happened to Bartimaeus. It may have happened like this. "Good morning, Bartimaeus!" A coin jingled in his cup. Before Bartimaeus could even call out his thank you, the friend shared his news.
"I've heard about a man in the country who some people say is the Messiah, the Promised One."
Immediately Bartimaeus was excited, too. "The Messiah! How can we be sure?" Bartimaeus wanted to know.
"Listen to this . . . He does miracles! He changed water into wine at a wedding — six big jars full! He has healed people who were sick. Cripples, and deaf and . . ."
Bartimaeus held his breath and waited for the next word.
". . . and blind!"
"Where is He?" Bartimaeus asked.
"He lives in Galilee. It is said He comes from Nazareth. He often comes to Jerusalem."
"I wonder, will He ever come to Jericho?"
"If He does, I'll be sure to let you know," his friend promised. "Goodbye, Bartimaeus."
"Wait! What is His name?" Bartimaeus wanted to know.
"Jesus. His name is Jesus." And the friend went on his way.

(Remove friend)

Bartimaeus knew about the Old Testament Scriptures (cf. Mark 10:48,49; Luke 18:38,39). He knew about the promised Messiah. He knew about the history of his people, the nation of Israel. That nation once had great kings; David and his son, Solomon. But the nation of Israel was not a great nation when Bartimaeus lived.
Bartimaeus and his friends expected that when the Messiah would come, He would make the nation great again. Was this man really the Messiah? Yes, this "miracle worker" must be the one. If so, He would be a descendant of King David.
The Lord Jesus Christ did come from the family of David. His mother Mary was of David's family. But more wonderful, Jesus Christ was the Son of God. God was His Father! Jesus, Son of God. Don't you love to say it? And, to think that He is your very personal friend. Or if He is not, He can become that this very day.
One morning Bartimaeus sat in his usual place near Jericho. Bartimaeus doubtless expected it to be just like any other morning. He held up his cup, expecting coins.
"Bakshish! Bakshish!" But no one paid any attention to him.

Scene 3
(Place figures of Christ and crowd, 2C-135, 2C-132 and 2C-134)

He began to realize that something was different. The noise? There was more noise than usual. Listening some more, Bartimaeus knew there was a big crowd of people coming down the road. What was going on? He must find out. The Bible says he asked about it.
"Somebody tell me, please, why all the noise? What are the people doing?" Bartimaeus questioned.
(Place man, 2C-136)

"Jesus, the man from Nazareth, is coming down the road. In a moment He will be going past you," someone told him.
Jesus of Nazareth! Jesus, Son of David! This was the moment for which he had been waiting.
"Jesus," he shouted. "Jesus, Son of David, have mercy on me."
"Bartimaeus, keep quiet!" Those who were in the front of the crowd sounded disgusted with him and spoke sharply.
Bartimaeus paid no attention to them. He shouted even louder. "Jesus, Son of David. Have mercy on me!"
The call of Bartimaeus reached the ears of the Lord Jesus. He stopped and stood still. "Call that man," He said. "Tell him to come to Me."
Possibly the very one who had been saying "keep quiet" was encouraging Bartimaeus now.
"Cheer up, Bartimaeus," he said. "It's all right. He's calling for you."

Scene 5 (same scene)
(Remove figures Bartimaeus, 2C-129, Christ, 2C-135. Place Christ, 2C-138 and Bartimaeus, 2C-137)

21

Bartimaeus had never been so excited. He threw off his coat and jumped to his feet. Perhaps someone guided him to the Lord Jesus. No doubt as Bartimaeus was moving toward the Lord Jesus, Jesus was moving toward him.

"What do you want Me to do for you?" the Lord Jesus asked.

"Oh, Lord, I want to see," Bartimaeus said.

"It shall be done," the Son of God answered. "Your faith — your belief in Me — has made you see."

(Exchange figure 2C-137 for 2C-139, Bartimaeus)

And, Bartimaeus did see! He looked into the face of the Lord Jesus first of all. What would it have been like to look into His face? Do you think Bartimaeus might have seen kindness in the eyes of the Lord? Do you think he could have seen a look of love in the face of Jesus, the perfect Son of God?

When the Lord Jesus looked into the face of Bartimaeus, what did He see? Surely He saw joy and love and trust in the face of the one who had been blind. The Bible says Bartimaeus praised and followed the Lord Jesus. ". . . he that followeth me shall not walk in darkness, but shall have the light of life" (John 8:12).

Light or darkness. Which do you choose? The sin in your life . . . lying, meanness, cheating, disobedience, selfishness, unbelief . . . would keep you out of Heaven. But, the Lord Jesus took the punishment for your sin when He died on the cross. If you receive the Lord Jesus as your Saviour from sin, and trust Him to forgive you, He will remove the darkness of sin from your life. Jesus Christ, the Light of Life, will come to live in you. Will you receive the Lord Jesus as your Saviour today? The Bible says, ". . . whoever shall call on the name of the Lord shall be saved" (Romans 10:13). Let me know if you would like to receive Him today. When class is over I want to show you in the Bible how you can know that you are saved. The Bible says when you receive Him you are no longer in darkness but in the light.

Jesus Christ will be your guide if you follow Him. How can He guide you? Through the Bible. It is from reading His Word and learning what it teaches that you can know what is right or wrong.

(Teacher: Choose some passage to illustrate. Verses from Mark 10 could be used.)

Read verses 35-37. What did James and John want? They wanted to be rulers. They wanted to be important.

Read 41. How did the other disciples feel? They were jealous. What did the Lord Jesus say was the right way? To be willing to serve others.

Simplify verse 42, read 43-45. What does it mean? To be great in the sight of God we should help others, not try to be more important than they are.)

This week I would like you to read Mark 10:13-16 at home. When you come back next time we'll talk about how Jesus showed the people the right way in those verses. *(Teacher: Give references to children so they remember. If some other passage is better for your group make your own selection. Before dismissing, give instruction for counseling children who may wish to receive Christ as Saviour today. See further helps under Application of the Truth.)*

LESSON TWELVE

MIRACLES AT CAPERNAUM
(Raising of Jairus' Daughter)

Scripture
Mark 5:21-43; Luke 8:40-56

Aim
That the child may trust the Lord Jesus to use His power to meet needs in his life.

Note to teacher:
The emphasis of these six lessons has been on the miracle working Christ. We want each student to know Him as one who has power to meet special needs in his life. We want the child to pray about his needs, expecting God to meet those needs, and be aware when He does. It is important that we help the children recognize God's part in the happenings in their lives, so that they see things as not mere coincidence, but as God working for them.

In order to accomplish this, some illustration of answered prayer is necessary. An illustration from your life will be much better than that from someone with whom they are not familiar, or some fictitious illustration. The following suggestions may bring to your attention some ways God has met your need as you trusted Him which you can share with your students:

Remembering something important . . . just in time!

Finding something you did not know you had, to meet an immediate and specific need.

Reading something that was just what you needed at that very time.

Learning of something which avoided an impending catastrophe.

Something which hindered you from doing an unwise thing.

Some instance where help came from an unexpected source at just the right moment.

Being guided to do the unusual which turned out to be God's perfect plan.

Memory Verse
Hebrews 13:8 — "Jesus Christ the same yesterday, and today, and forever."

Teaching the Memory Verse
What is a word in our verse which means *past? present? future?* (Use chart here described under Visual Aids. *Write* in *yesterday, today,* and *forever* on chart)

We have been studying the life of Jesus Christ. Into which part of the verse would you place the things we have been learning about Him? What was He like then? (This should initiate some good discussion. Make sure that in connection with His power the students understand that He was a loving, caring person.) It is not hard for us to understand the Lord Jesus will be *the same* in the forever future. But, is He the same today? Can He use His power to do special things for you today? (Do not become too involved in answering this as the answer will be found during the teaching of the lesson.)

Suggested Songs
Salvation Songs Number 1: "Only Believe," No. 59; "There's Nothing Too Hard for Thee," No. 65; "The Light of the World Is Jesus," No. 99

Salvation Songs Number 2: "Yesterday, Today, Forever," No. 46; "John 1:12," No. 79

Salvation Songs Number 3: "Blind Eyes Jesus Made to See," No. 20

Review Questions
(Note these questions are related to all lessons in this Volume, and are designed to emphasize the miracles therein. Add the miracles mentioned to your chart under "yesterday.")

1. What was the first miracle performed by the Lord Jesus?
A. He turned water into wine.

2. Do you remember what lesson we learned from that miracle?
A. The Lord Jesus can help us when we have problems.
3. What important man in Jerusalem came to the Lord Jesus because he saw the miracles Jesus did?
A. Nicodemus.
4. What miracle happened to that man?
A. He was born again.
5. One day the Lord Jesus did something His disciples did not understand, which resulted in a miracle. What did He do?
A. He went through Samaria and talked with a Samaritan woman.
6. What miracle took place because of this?
A. The woman received the Lord Jesus and brought her friends to Him.
7. What miracle did the Lord Jesus perform for a father?
A. He healed his little son.
8. What other miracle happened in that home?
A. Everyone who lived at that house trusted the Lord Jesus.
9. What miracle took place for the beggar from Jericho?
A. He was blind and Jesus gave him sight.
10. What miracle can remove the darkness of sin from our lives?
A. The death and resurrection of the Lord Jesus when we trust Him. Discuss what the children found in the Bible research assigned last week.

Schedule for Teaching
Song — "The Light of the World Is Jesus"
Song — "Blind Eyes Jesus Made to See"
Teach Memory Verse — Hebrews 13:8
Song — "Yesterday, Today, Forever"
Review Questions
Song — "There's Nothing Too Hard for Thee"
Song — "Only Believe"
Lesson — "Miracles at Capernaum"
Application of Truth

Visual Aids
Seaside and Indoor flannel scenes; figures 2C-140 — 2C-156
Prepare a chart from sheet of poster board or newsprint. Rule three columns with headings "past," "present," "future." Allow space near these headings for writing in "yesterday," "today," "forever" during teaching of the memory verse. During review time, add items under "yesterday" as children think of the things Jesus did while on earth. In applying the truth, add items to section "today" as you discuss how God works in our lives now. Also add the truths under "forever" as outlined in text at conclusion of lesson.
For take-home items, prepare charts for children from 8½ x 11 sheets. Children may fill in the "yesterday" and "forever" truths from your chart, but encourage their filling in "today" truth as they trust the Lord for a specific need this week.

Lesson
What is a miracle? We have used that word over and over again in our lessons about the Lord Jesus. *(Initiate some discussion here.)* The dictionary says it is "a wonderful thing." It is a happening that is different from the way things are expected to happen. I remember a very special thing God did for me one time ... (Teacher, use some personal illustration as suggested under *Note to Teacher.)*
Can God do special things for you? He did some things for you this very week. We'll be talking more about that later today. If you are not sure how the Lord Jesus can meet needs in your life, this lesson can help you find out.

Scene 1 (seaside scene)
A new day began in the town of Capernaum. It was just an ordinary day for most people. They ate their breakfast. They went to their work.

(Place 2C-140, 2C-141, crowd)

But, many people were watching the lake. They were expecting the Lord Jesus to return to their city that day. They were eager to have Him come. Could that be His boat in the distance? Yes, it was. "He's coming. He's coming. Jesus is coming!" They probably called to one another.
Quickly the people started to gather by the shore. The word spread into the city. "Jesus is coming."
A woman slowly left her house. She was so weak. It was hard for her to walk. She had been sick for twelve years. She had gone to doctor after doctor. She had spent much money. But, still she was sick. It seems as if she was very much alone. Perhaps she had no family nor friends. Wouldn't it be hard to be sick and have no one to care? Families and friends who care are one of God's gifts to us.
The woman was not quite sure what she would do when she did see the Lord Jesus. She was a bit scared. She did not just want to walk up to Him and ask Him to heal her. She wondered how she would be able to get through that crowd. Was something special going to happen for her today?
(On small board held in hand, show figures 2C-142 and 143, Jairus and wife)

At another house in Capernaum a father and mother were greatly worried. Their only child, a daughter twelve years old, was dreadfully sick. The doctors had done all they could. Her parents were afraid she was going to die. No wonder they were troubled. Then, they heard the news.
(Place figures, 2C-144 Christ, and disciples, 2C-145 on seaside scene)

"Jesus has come. He's down by the lake."
Perhaps the mother said, "Go quickly! Ask Him to come. He's the only one who can make her well." And that father, Jairus, hurried as fast as he could.
(Remove small board and place 2C-146, Jairus)

Was something special going to happen for that family today? The sight of the crowd could have made Jairus lose hope. Would he ever be able to get to Jesus in time? He was sure there were many sick people in the crowd. Every one of them would want the attention of the Lord Jesus. Jairus began pushing through the crowd. People looked. Oh! Jairus was an important man. He was one of the rulers of the synagogue. Perhaps they moved aside to let him through. They may have been surprised that Jairus wanted to come to Jesus for help. Most of the leaders at the synagogue had no time for the Lord Jesus because they did not believe He was the Son of God. As Jairus reached the Lord Jesus, he bowed low before Him.
(Remove 2C-146, Jairus; place 2C-147. Remove 2C-144; place 2C-148, Christ)

"My daughter is about to die," he said. "Come, lay Your hands on her so that she may get well and live." Jairus earnestly begged the Lord Jesus.
The Lord did not hesitate. Perhaps He said, "I will come. You lead the way."
(Remove 2C-147 and 2C-148. Place 2C-144 and 2C-146, Christ and Jairus)

Jairus started off toward his house as fast as he could go and Jesus followed. The crowd followed, too.

While they were on the way, the sick woman who started out to reach the Lord Jesus was getting closer and closer to Him. "I believe," she said to herself, "if I can just touch His robe, I'll be healed." Timidly she reached out her hand and touched the fringe of His robe. Instantly she was healed! She could feel that she was well. What joy filled her heart!
Suddenly the Lord Jesus stopped and looked around. "Who touched me?" He asked.
"I didn't." "I didn't." "Not I." "I did not touch You." The answers were coming from the crowd. No one was moving now. Jairus stopped and stood waiting.
(Remove 2C-146. Place 2C-149, Jairus)

"But Master," said the disciple Peter, "the crowds are jamming and pushing and shoving You. And You ask, 'Who touched me?' There are people everywhere. Dozens of people must be touching You." The other disciples agreed with Peter.
"Not like that," explained the Lord Jesus. "I felt power pass from Me and I know someone touched Me and received help." And still, Jairus stood waiting.
Do you think the Lord Jesus knew who touched Him? Certainly He did. Then, why did He ask? I believe He wanted the woman to say what He had done for her. He must have wanted the crowd to know, too, that He cared about one woman's need. Something very special had happened to her. Jesus used His power to meet her need. It was really a miracle.
What is the greatest miracle that could ever happen to you? (Discussion time. Remind class of greatest miracle — receiving forgiveness of sin.) Has the Lord Jesus forgiven your sin and given you a new kind of life? Sin spoils your life. You and I were born sinners (Psalm 51:5). Because we are sinners, we lie and cheat and are often mean and selfish, think wicked thoughts and say unkind words. The Lord Jesus said our hearts are sinful. Sinful things come from within us (Matthew 15:19). Sin must be punished. The punishment of sin is death. God Himself set the punishment. Still, God loves us, and sent His Son, the Lord Jesus Christ, to take the punishment for sin. Receiving forgiveness for sin is the greatest miracle that could ever take place.
If God has done that very special miracle for you He wants you to tell about it. The Lord Jesus wants you to tell that He died and rose from the dead so that your sin could be forgiven. Have you told anyone? He loves to hear you tell what He has done for you. He waited for the woman to tell what had happened to her.
(Place 2C-150, woman, in front of Jesus)

She stepped out from the crowd. "It was I who touched You," she said, and trembling she knelt at His feet. Then, she told her story.

The Lord Jesus spoke kindly to her. Because the woman had trusted in Him she was made well from her sickness.

All this time Jairus still stood waiting. *Why does He not hurry?* He must have been thinking. *If only that woman had waited. If she had been sick twelve years a bit more time would not have made that much difference.* How hard it was to wait! Jairus was afraid his daughter would not live much longer.

There are times when you pray and ask God to do something for you. He does not do it right away. For some reason He wants you to wait. And, you are troubled because you cannot see what He has planned to do.

Janie had a habit of begging her parents to do something or get her something NOW. "Not now," Mother or Dad would say.

"But, when?" Janie wanted to know.

Usually Mother or Dad had a plan in mind for her so they answered, "Oh, sometime."

"Oh, yes, sometime!" Janie exclaimed impatiently, beginning to pout. She didn't understand that her parents knew what was best for her.

If God would *always* give you what you ask immediately, His perfect plan would be spoiled. You have to wait for His right time. You think your need is right now, but God knows better. The special thing He has planned for you is far better than the thing you asked for. Jairus did not know about God's better plan for his need as he stood waiting.

(Place servant, 2C-151)

Suddenly, Jairus saw someone pushing through the crowd. Someone from his house . . . Jairus' heart seemed to stop. He was afraid to hear the message.

"I've just come from your house. Your daughter is dead. You need not trouble the Master anymore."

Poor Jairus. All hope was gone. It was too late now. If only they had not been detained. He looked at the Lord Jesus, and the Lord Jesus was looking at him.

"Don't be afraid," He said. "Only believe. Just trust. She will get well."

Jairus must have thought that the Lord Jesus really did not understand. How could his daughter get well if she was dead? But again Jairus led the way to his home.

(Remove 2C-149; place 2C-146)

The Lord Jesus followed. The crowd followed, too.

(Remove all figures)

When they reached the house they found it filled with people. Weeping . . . wailing . . . playing sad music on flutes . . . groaning . . . loud crying!

"Stop all this fuss," Jesus said. "She's only sleeping." He meant He could awaken her out of death just as if she had been asleep. They laughed in His face.

"She's dead," they said. They thought He could do nothing about it.

The Lord Jesus sent all those unbelieving people out of the house. The only disciples with Him now were Peter, James and John. Then, with the mother, and father, they went into the room where the young girl lay.

Scene 2 (indoor scene)
(Place Christ, disciples, parents and child, 2C-148, 145, 149, 143, 152, 153)

No longer were her cheeks red with the high fever. She was white and still and cold. The Lord Jesus reached out and took one of her cold hands in his.

"Little girl, get up," He said.

Jairus watched. He tried to believe what he heard. Then it happened! His daughter opened her eyes! She sat up! She got out of bed and walked! She probably ran into her mother's arms.

(Remove 2C-153; place 154. Remove 2C-149 and 143. Place 2C-155 and 156)

Jairus and his wife had never been so surprised or thrilled or happy.

Which would have been the greater miracle, to heal the little girl while she was sick, or to raise her from the dead? Of course, the greater miracle was to bring her back from the dead. But, Jairus had not known what the Lord Jesus had planned.

"Give her something to eat," the Lord Jesus said. She had been sick a long time. Now she was well. She would be hungry and she needed food.

Did you know that you were once dead? The Bible says "You . . . were dead in . . . sin." But, if you have received the Lord Jesus, this same verse says God made you alive (Ephesians 2:1 — "quickened" means "made alive"). To be made alive from being dead in sin is a very wonderful thing. We have thought about past miracles for you, especially the death of the Lord Jesus on the cross and His resurrection from the dead so that He could be your Saviour from sin. But what does He do for you today? God does many wonderful things for you, but perhaps many times you are not aware of the way He works in your life.

A teacher told her class of something special God did for her. "Oh," said Beth, "that was just good luck." The teacher explained that when you belong to God, through trusting the Lord Jesus, God works for you. Things do not happen because of good or bad luck, but because God is working in your life. When you learn to know more about the Lord, it is easy to see that He does special things for you. As you read His Word you see how He helped people at that time. You remember those things as you think about Him at school, or at home, or at play. You begin to realize how He has helped you, too.

The boys and girls received their report cards from school on Good News Club® day. They were excitedly discussing their grades. "God helped me to get a good grade in that spelling test," Lisa announced. "And He helped me get six A's and three B's," said Lee.

Were the Good News Clubbers learning to recognize the way God worked for them? Can you think of some thing He can do for you? (Discussion . . . listing the things they suggest on chart under *Today*. Teacher may direct discussion to victory over sins and problems such as lying, fighting, disobedience, etc.) Ask the Lord to help you recognize that which He does especially for you.

Our verse says, "Jesus Christ the same yesterday, and today, and forever." There is a miracle which has not yet happened. (Add items to chart under *forever*.) The Lord Jesus is coming again. He is coming for you who belong to Him. There is the miracle of Heaven. And, the miracle of life forever. Our bodies will one day die. But, if you've trusted the Lord Jesus as your Saviour, the real you will live forever with God in Heaven. God has so many special things planned for the future. Most of them will be surprises such as we could never imagine.

Let's thank Him for using His power to meet our needs and do special things for us! *(Teacher, permit audible prayers or give opportunity for silent prayer.)*

If you have not yet received the Lord Jesus, tell Him what is in your heart right now. Tell Him you know you have sinned, but you believe He died and rose again for you. Tell Him you receive Him right now for the forgiveness of your sins. If you have done that today for the first time, or would like to, will you lift your hand so that I may know about it, too? I would like to talk with you after class to make sure that you understand, and show you some promises from God's Word.

(Teacher . . . it would be most effective if you could make up a simple chart for the child to take home, like the one you worked on in class. Tell him to write in the "yesterday" and "forever" like yours, but to fill in the "today" this week as he trusts God for a specific need in his life.)

As we leave class today let's go thanking Him that He is the same yesterday and today and forever.

(Sing — "Yesterday, Today, Forever" and remind children of place to meet you for further counsel. See Application of Truth.)

My God is so great, so strong and so mighty. There's nothing my God cannot do.

God's love is so great and I know He loves me, For He gave His Son for my sin.

My God Is So Great

1st stanza: Traditional
2nd stanza: Elsie Lippy

Traditional

1. My God is so great, so strong and so mighty There's nothing my God cannot do! My God is so great, so strong and so mighty There's nothing my God cannot do! The mountains are His, The rivers are His, The stars are His handiwork too. My God is so great, so strong and so mighty There's nothing my God cannot do!

2. God's love is so great, and I know He loves me, For He gave His Son for my sin. God's love is so great, and I know He loves me, For He gave His Son for my sin. Christ died for me, He rose again, He's coming back for me, too. God's love is so great, and I know He loves me, For He gave His Son for my sin.

2nd stanza Copyright © 1981 by Child Evangelism Fellowship Inc. All rights reserved.

Dot to Dot Lesson Review

Prepare a poster with dots as shown.

The object of this review is to form boxes by connecting dots and placing the initial of one of the 12 disciples in the box.

To play: Divide children into two teams. Use a different colored marker for each team. When a child answers a review question correctly he connects two dots anywhere on the board and receives 50 points for his team. If he adds the last line to complete a box and can place the initial of a disciple in the box his team receives an additional 100 points (a total of 150.) If he cannot name a disciple, he still receives 50 points for completing the box. Team with the most completed boxes with disciples wins. After completing the review, sing "There Were 12 Disciples."

Variations:
1. Place Bible stickers inside the dotted sections. The person adding the final line to a box receives 100 extra points for his team if he can quote a Bible verse.

2. Place stickers of Bible miracles inside the dotted sections. If the child who completes a dotted section can name a Bible miracle, he fills in the square with the marker, gaining an additional 100 points for his team. or name a miracle in the Bible.

3. Define a miracle as an amazing, wonderful thing only God can do because He is all-powerful. Encourage teams ahead of time to plan how to act out one of the miracles for the other team to guess. This variation should be saved until Lessons 5 and 6 so children are familiar with several Bible miracles. Awarding 1000 points for each charade and a round of applause for participants will bring reward.

How to Lead a Child to Christ

1. Show him his NEED of salvation; that all persons are not going to Heaven; that no one in himself is good enough to go and the result of sin is forever separation from God (Romans 3:23; Revelation 21:27; John 8:21,24).
2. Show him the WAY of salvation. Salvation is a free gift because the Lord Jesus took our place on the cross, was buried and rose again from the dead (John 3:16; Ephesians 2:8; 1 Corinthians 15:3, 4).
3. Lead him to RECEIVE the gift of salvation, even Jesus Christ, by trusting Him as his personal Savior (John 1:12; Revelation 3:20).
4. From the Word of God, help him find ASSURANCE of his salvation (John 3:36; Revelation 3:20; Hebrews 13:5).
5. Lead him to CONFESS Christ (Matthew 10:32). This confession should be made to you, other workers, later to his friends and as circumstances permit, in a public church service.

How to Lead a Child in Consecration

1. Question the child relative to his salvation, giving him opportunity to confess Christ to you. If he does not show clarity on this point, he is not ready for consecration. Go over with him the steps given in leading a child to Christ.
2. If he is clear on the reality of his salvation, lead him to give himself to God today by fully obeying what he knows God wants him to do (Romans 12:1 or 1 Corinthians 6:19, 20).
3. Show him that the Holy Spirit who lives in him will make known to him through the Word of God what He wants him to do each day (John 14:26); e.g. obey parents (Colossians 3:20), witness for Christ where he is (Acts 1:8), set aside a time for reading the Bible and prayer (1 Timothy 2:1-5; 4:15; 2 Timothy 2:15), live every part of his life to please God (1 Timothy 4:12).
4. Now that you have talked these things over with the child lead him in a prayer of dedication: "Dear Lord Jesus, today I give myself to You. I want You to take control of my life. Help me to live each day to please You. Help me to be faithful in reading Your Word that I may know Your plan for me." Lead the child in a prayer of thanks.
5. Help the child to see that it is a sin for him to take control again of his own life, and that when he sins, he should confess it to God, trusting Him to forgive. He then should allow God to once more take control of his life (1 John 1:9; Proverbs 3:5, 6).

Hebrews 13:8
Jesus Christ the same yesterday, and today, and forever.